THE 100+ SERIES™

Reproducible Activities

Timed Math Tests

Helping Students Achieve Their Personal Best

Addition and Subtraction

by
Patricia Howard

**Cover Design
by
Jeff Van Kanegan**

**Inside Art
by
Tim Foley**

Published by Instructional Fair
an imprint of
Frank Schaffer Publications®

Instructional Fair

Frank Schaffer Publications®

Instructional Fair is an imprint of Frank Schaffer Publications.

Send all inquiries to:
Frank Schaffer Publications
8720 Orion Place
Columbus, Ohio 43240-2111

Timed Math Tests–Addition and Subtraction

ISBN 0-7424-0226-6

5 6 7 8 9 10 MAZ 09 08

Table of Contents

3

Introduction

It is necessary that students have been taught and understand the concepts of addition and subtraction before beginning the activities in this book. Rather than teaching concepts, the objective of this book is to offer students the opportunity to practice and commit to memory their addition and subtraction facts and to challenge them to reach for their personal best. These tests are designed to be repeated by students until the desired speed and accuracy is reached.

Suggested Uses for This Book:

- Have students write in a time goal for each test. Record students' progress with the record chart. Provide each student with a copy of the chart to keep track of his or her own scores.

- Give students the opportunity to assess and evaluate their work and to set their own goals by completing a self-evaluation of their progress each week. Reward students for perfect scores or for meeting personal goals.

- Send home the Web site suggestions and math games included below. Try to include parents in your students' learning of their math facts. Practice at home can be valuable to making the learning of math facts a stress-free experience.

Web Sites and Software

www.edu4kids.com/math

Features electronic flash cards of basic math facts with difficulty levels ranging from two up to ten numbers in a problem

www.funbrain.com

Features interactive games for practice of addition, subtraction, and more

www.aplusmath.com

Flashcards, worksheets, and interactive games

Home and Classroom Games

Snap Facts: 2 players; deck of playing cards with face cards removed

Deal the cards between two players. Each player places his or her card stack facedown. Players draw cards from their stacks at the same time and place them face up on the table. The first player to add the two cards together is the winner and keeps the two cards. The player with the most cards wins.

Rolling Along: 2 players; a pair of dice

Players take turns rolling the two dice and adding or subtracting the two numbers. Play for a specified period of time and keep score. The highest score wins.

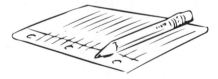

Addition Record Chart

Test	Time	Score	Time	Score
+2A				
+2B				
+2C				
+3A				
+3B				
+3C				
+4A				
+4B				
+4C				
+5A				
+5B				
+5C				
+6A				
+6B				
+6C				
+7A				
+7B				
+7C				
+8A				
+8B				
+8C				
+9A				
+9B				
+9C				
+10A				
+10B				
+10C				
+11A				
+11B				
+11C				
+12A				
+12B				
+12C				

IF87115 *Timed Math Tests*

© Frank Schaffer Publications

Addition Record Chart (cont.)

Test	Time	Score	Time	Score
+13A				
+13B				
+13C				
+14A				
+14B				
+14C				
+15A				
+15B				
+15C				
+16A				
+16B				
+16C				
+17A				
+17B				
+17C				
+18A				
+18B				
+18C				
+19A				
+19B				
+19C				
Review A				
Review B				
Review C				
Review D				

IF87115 *Timed Math Tests*

Addition Pretest

+2A

Name _____   Date _____

Time _____   Score _____

My time goal is _____ .

1.
$$9 + 2$$

2.
$$2 + 2$$

3.
$$20 + 2$$

4.
$$18 + 2$$

5.
$$11 + 2$$

6.
$$10 + 2$$

7.
$$15 + 2$$

8.
$$4 + 2$$

9.
$$14 + 2$$

10.
$$19 + 2$$

11.
$$5 + 2$$

12.
$$13 + 2$$

13.
$$7 + 2$$

14.
$$1 + 2$$

15.
$$3 + 2$$

16.
$$17 + 2$$

17.
$$6 + 2$$

18.
$$12 + 2$$

19.
$$16 + 2$$

20.
$$8 + 2$$

IF87115 *Timed Math Tests*

Addition Practice

Name _____   Date _____

Time _____   Score _____

My time goal is _____.

1.
$$\begin{array}{r} 2 \\ + 8 \\ \hline \end{array}$$

2.
$$\begin{array}{r} 2 \\ + 16 \\ \hline \end{array}$$

3.
$$\begin{array}{r} 2 \\ + 12 \\ \hline \end{array}$$

4.
$$\begin{array}{r} 2 \\ + 6 \\ \hline \end{array}$$

5.
$$\begin{array}{r} 2 \\ + 17 \\ \hline \end{array}$$

6.
$$\begin{array}{r} 2 \\ + 3 \\ \hline \end{array}$$

7.
$$\begin{array}{r} 2 \\ + 1 \\ \hline \end{array}$$

8.
$$\begin{array}{r} 2 \\ + 7 \\ \hline \end{array}$$

9.
$$\begin{array}{r} 2 \\ + 13 \\ \hline \end{array}$$

10.
$$\begin{array}{r} 2 \\ + 5 \\ \hline \end{array}$$

11.
$$\begin{array}{r} 2 \\ + 19 \\ \hline \end{array}$$

12.
$$\begin{array}{r} 2 \\ + 14 \\ \hline \end{array}$$

13.
$$\begin{array}{r} 2 \\ + 4 \\ \hline \end{array}$$

14.
$$\begin{array}{r} 2 \\ + 15 \\ \hline \end{array}$$

15.
$$\begin{array}{r} 2 \\ + 10 \\ \hline \end{array}$$

16.
$$\begin{array}{r} 2 \\ + 11 \\ \hline \end{array}$$

17.
$$\begin{array}{r} 2 \\ + 18 \\ \hline \end{array}$$

18.
$$\begin{array}{r} 2 \\ + 20 \\ \hline \end{array}$$

19.
$$\begin{array}{r} 2 \\ + 2 \\ \hline \end{array}$$

20.
$$\begin{array}{r} 2 \\ + 9 \\ \hline \end{array}$$

IF87115 *Timed Math Tests*

Addition Challenge

Name _____   Date _____

Time _____   Score _____

🕐 My time goal is _____ .

1.
$$\begin{array}{r} \square \\ +\ 2 \\ \hline 21 \end{array}$$

2.
$$\begin{array}{r} \square \\ +\ 2 \\ \hline 14 \end{array}$$

3.
$$\begin{array}{r} \square \\ +\ 2 \\ \hline 10 \end{array}$$

4.
$$\begin{array}{r} \square \\ +\ 2 \\ \hline 6 \end{array}$$

5.
$$\begin{array}{r} \square \\ +\ 2 \\ \hline 12 \end{array}$$

6.
$$\begin{array}{r} \square \\ +\ 2 \\ \hline 4 \end{array}$$

7.
$$\begin{array}{r} \square \\ +\ 2 \\ \hline 16 \end{array}$$

8.
$$\begin{array}{r} \square \\ +\ 2 \\ \hline 2 \end{array}$$

9.
$$\begin{array}{r} \square \\ +\ 2 \\ \hline 8 \end{array}$$

10.
$$\begin{array}{r} \square \\ +\ 2 \\ \hline 18 \end{array}$$

11.
$$\begin{array}{r} \square \\ +\ 2 \\ \hline 20 \end{array}$$

12.
$$\begin{array}{r} \square \\ +\ 2 \\ \hline 11 \end{array}$$

13.
$$\begin{array}{r} \square \\ +\ 2 \\ \hline 3 \end{array}$$

14.
$$\begin{array}{r} \square \\ +\ 2 \\ \hline 15 \end{array}$$

15.
$$\begin{array}{r} \square \\ +\ 2 \\ \hline 9 \end{array}$$

16.
$$\begin{array}{r} \square \\ +\ 2 \\ \hline 7 \end{array}$$

17.
$$\begin{array}{r} \square \\ +\ 2 \\ \hline 19 \end{array}$$

18.
$$\begin{array}{r} \square \\ +\ 2 \\ \hline 5 \end{array}$$

19.
$$\begin{array}{r} \square \\ +\ 2 \\ \hline 13 \end{array}$$

20.
$$\begin{array}{r} \square \\ +\ 2 \\ \hline 17 \end{array}$$

IF87115 *Timed Math Tests*

Addition Pretest

Name _____   Date _____

Time _____   Score _____

🕐 My time goal is _____ .

1. $\begin{array}{r} 17 \\ +\ 3 \\ \hline \end{array}$	2. $\begin{array}{r} 19 \\ +\ 3 \\ \hline \end{array}$	3. $\begin{array}{r} 4 \\ +\ 3 \\ \hline \end{array}$	4. $\begin{array}{r} 6 \\ +\ 3 \\ \hline \end{array}$	5. $\begin{array}{r} 2 \\ +\ 3 \\ \hline \end{array}$
6. $\begin{array}{r} 8 \\ +\ 3 \\ \hline \end{array}$	7. $\begin{array}{r} 10 \\ +\ 3 \\ \hline \end{array}$	8. $\begin{array}{r} 16 \\ +\ 3 \\ \hline \end{array}$	9. $\begin{array}{r} 5 \\ +\ 3 \\ \hline \end{array}$	10. $\begin{array}{r} 14 \\ +\ 3 \\ \hline \end{array}$
11. $\begin{array}{r} 7 \\ +\ 3 \\ \hline \end{array}$	12. $\begin{array}{r} 20 \\ +\ 3 \\ \hline \end{array}$	13. $\begin{array}{r} 15 \\ +\ 3 \\ \hline \end{array}$	14. $\begin{array}{r} 12 \\ +\ 3 \\ \hline \end{array}$	15. $\begin{array}{r} 18 \\ +\ 3 \\ \hline \end{array}$
16. $\begin{array}{r} 9 \\ +\ 3 \\ \hline \end{array}$	17. $\begin{array}{r} 3 \\ +\ 3 \\ \hline \end{array}$	18. $\begin{array}{r} 1 \\ +\ 3 \\ \hline \end{array}$	19. $\begin{array}{r} 11 \\ +\ 3 \\ \hline \end{array}$	20. $\begin{array}{r} 13 \\ +\ 3 \\ \hline \end{array}$

IF87115 *Timed Math Tests*

Addition Practice

Name _____ Date _____

Time _____ Score _____

🕐 My time goal is _____ .

1. $\begin{array}{r} 3 \\ + 7 \\ \hline \end{array}$
2. $\begin{array}{r} 3 \\ + 17 \\ \hline \end{array}$
3. $\begin{array}{r} 3 \\ + 20 \\ \hline \end{array}$
4. $\begin{array}{r} 3 \\ + 15 \\ \hline \end{array}$
5. $\begin{array}{r} 3 \\ + 12 \\ \hline \end{array}$

6. $\begin{array}{r} 3 \\ + 18 \\ \hline \end{array}$
7. $\begin{array}{r} 3 \\ + 3 \\ \hline \end{array}$
8. $\begin{array}{r} 3 \\ + 1 \\ \hline \end{array}$
9. $\begin{array}{r} 3 \\ + 11 \\ \hline \end{array}$
10. $\begin{array}{r} 3 \\ + 13 \\ \hline \end{array}$

11. $\begin{array}{r} 3 \\ + 14 \\ \hline \end{array}$
12. $\begin{array}{r} 3 \\ + 5 \\ \hline \end{array}$
13. $\begin{array}{r} 3 \\ + 16 \\ \hline \end{array}$
14. $\begin{array}{r} 3 \\ + 10 \\ \hline \end{array}$
15. $\begin{array}{r} 3 \\ + 8 \\ \hline \end{array}$

16. $\begin{array}{r} 3 \\ + 2 \\ \hline \end{array}$
17. $\begin{array}{r} 3 \\ + 6 \\ \hline \end{array}$
18. $\begin{array}{r} 3 \\ + 4 \\ \hline \end{array}$
19. $\begin{array}{r} 3 \\ + 19 \\ \hline \end{array}$
20. $\begin{array}{r} 3 \\ + 9 \\ \hline \end{array}$

IF87115 *Timed Math Tests*

Name _____ Date _____

Time _____ Score _____

🕐 My time goal is _____ .

1.
$$\begin{array}{r} \square \\ + 3 \\ \hline 9 \end{array}$$

2.
$$\begin{array}{r} \square \\ + 3 \\ \hline 19 \end{array}$$

3.
$$\begin{array}{r} \square \\ + 3 \\ \hline 12 \end{array}$$

4.
$$\begin{array}{r} \square \\ + 3 \\ \hline 3 \end{array}$$

5.
$$\begin{array}{r} \square \\ + 3 \\ \hline 5 \end{array}$$

6.
$$\begin{array}{r} \square \\ + 3 \\ \hline 7 \end{array}$$

7.
$$\begin{array}{r} \square \\ + 3 \\ \hline 11 \end{array}$$

8.
$$\begin{array}{r} \square \\ + 3 \\ \hline 4 \end{array}$$

9.
$$\begin{array}{r} \square \\ + 3 \\ \hline 20 \end{array}$$

10.
$$\begin{array}{r} \square \\ + 3 \\ \hline 6 \end{array}$$

11.
$$\begin{array}{r} \square \\ + 3 \\ \hline 18 \end{array}$$

12.
$$\begin{array}{r} \square \\ + 3 \\ \hline 15 \end{array}$$

13.
$$\begin{array}{r} \square \\ + 3 \\ \hline 11 \end{array}$$

14.
$$\begin{array}{r} \square \\ + 3 \\ \hline 13 \end{array}$$

15.
$$\begin{array}{r} \square \\ + 3 \\ \hline 10 \end{array}$$

16.
$$\begin{array}{r} \square \\ + 3 \\ \hline 16 \end{array}$$

17.
$$\begin{array}{r} \square \\ + 3 \\ \hline 14 \end{array}$$

18.
$$\begin{array}{r} \square \\ + 3 \\ \hline 17 \end{array}$$

19.
$$\begin{array}{r} \square \\ + 3 \\ \hline 8 \end{array}$$

20.
$$\begin{array}{r} \square \\ + 3 \\ \hline 7 \end{array}$$

IF87115 *Timed Math Tests*

Addition Pretest

+4A

Name _____   Date _____

Time _____   Score _____

My time goal is _____ .

1.
$$20 \\ +\ 4$$

2.
$$5 \\ +\ 4$$

3.
$$9 \\ +\ 4$$

4.
$$11 \\ +\ 4$$

5.
$$7 \\ +\ 4$$

6.
$$15 \\ +\ 4$$

7.
$$3 \\ +\ 4$$

8.
$$18 \\ +\ 4$$

9.
$$12 \\ +\ 4$$

10.
$$4 \\ +\ 4$$

11.
$$16 \\ +\ 4$$

12.
$$1 \\ +\ 4$$

13.
$$8 \\ +\ 4$$

14.
$$14 \\ +\ 4$$

15.
$$19 \\ +\ 4$$

16.
$$6 \\ +\ 4$$

17.
$$10 \\ +\ 4$$

18.
$$13 \\ +\ 4$$

19.
$$17 \\ +\ 4$$

20.
$$2 \\ +\ 4$$

IF87115 *Timed Math Tests*

Addition Practice

Name _____ Date _____

Time _____ Score _____

My time goal is _____ .

1.
$$\begin{array}{r} 4 \\ +\ 2 \\ \hline \end{array}$$

2.
$$\begin{array}{r} 4 \\ +\ 17 \\ \hline \end{array}$$

3.
$$\begin{array}{r} 4 \\ +\ 13 \\ \hline \end{array}$$

4.
$$\begin{array}{r} 4 \\ +\ 10 \\ \hline \end{array}$$

5.
$$\begin{array}{r} 4 \\ +\ 6 \\ \hline \end{array}$$

6.
$$\begin{array}{r} 4 \\ +\ 19 \\ \hline \end{array}$$

7.
$$\begin{array}{r} 4 \\ +\ 14 \\ \hline \end{array}$$

8.
$$\begin{array}{r} 4 \\ +\ 8 \\ \hline \end{array}$$

9.
$$\begin{array}{r} 4 \\ +\ 1 \\ \hline \end{array}$$

10.
$$\begin{array}{r} 4 \\ +\ 16 \\ \hline \end{array}$$

11.
$$\begin{array}{r} 4 \\ +\ 4 \\ \hline \end{array}$$

12.
$$\begin{array}{r} 4 \\ +\ 12 \\ \hline \end{array}$$

13.
$$\begin{array}{r} 4 \\ +\ 18 \\ \hline \end{array}$$

14.
$$\begin{array}{r} 4 \\ +\ 3 \\ \hline \end{array}$$

15.
$$\begin{array}{r} 4 \\ +\ 15 \\ \hline \end{array}$$

16.
$$\begin{array}{r} 4 \\ +\ 7 \\ \hline \end{array}$$

17.
$$\begin{array}{r} 4 \\ +\ 11 \\ \hline \end{array}$$

18.
$$\begin{array}{r} 4 \\ +\ 9 \\ \hline \end{array}$$

19.
$$\begin{array}{r} 4 \\ +\ 5 \\ \hline \end{array}$$

20.
$$\begin{array}{r} 4 \\ +\ 20 \\ \hline \end{array}$$

Addition Challenge

Name _____   Date _____

Time _____   Score _____

🕐 My time goal is _____ .

1.
$$\begin{array}{r} \square \\ +\ 4 \\ \hline 21 \end{array}$$

2.
$$\begin{array}{r} \square \\ +\ 4 \\ \hline 14 \end{array}$$

3.
$$\begin{array}{r} \square \\ +\ 4 \\ \hline 10 \end{array}$$

4.
$$\begin{array}{r} \square \\ +\ 4 \\ \hline 6 \end{array}$$

5.
$$\begin{array}{r} \square \\ +\ 4 \\ \hline 12 \end{array}$$

6.
$$\begin{array}{r} \square \\ +\ 4 \\ \hline 24 \end{array}$$

7.
$$\begin{array}{r} \square \\ +\ 4 \\ \hline 16 \end{array}$$

8.
$$\begin{array}{r} \square \\ +\ 4 \\ \hline 22 \end{array}$$

9.
$$\begin{array}{r} \square \\ +\ 4 \\ \hline 8 \end{array}$$

10.
$$\begin{array}{r} \square \\ +\ 4 \\ \hline 18 \end{array}$$

11.
$$\begin{array}{r} \square \\ +\ 4 \\ \hline 20 \end{array}$$

12.
$$\begin{array}{r} \square \\ +\ 4 \\ \hline 11 \end{array}$$

13.
$$\begin{array}{r} \square \\ +\ 4 \\ \hline 23 \end{array}$$

14.
$$\begin{array}{r} \square \\ +\ 4 \\ \hline 15 \end{array}$$

15.
$$\begin{array}{r} \square \\ +\ 4 \\ \hline 9 \end{array}$$

16.
$$\begin{array}{r} \square \\ +\ 4 \\ \hline 7 \end{array}$$

17.
$$\begin{array}{r} \square \\ +\ 4 \\ \hline 19 \end{array}$$

18.
$$\begin{array}{r} \square \\ +\ 4 \\ \hline 5 \end{array}$$

19.
$$\begin{array}{r} \square \\ +\ 4 \\ \hline 13 \end{array}$$

20.
$$\begin{array}{r} \square \\ +\ 4 \\ \hline 17 \end{array}$$

IF87115 *Timed Math Tests*

Addition Pretest

Name _____ Date _____

Time _____ Score _____

My time goal is _____ .

1.
$$\begin{array}{r} 2 \\ +\ 5 \\ \hline \end{array}$$

2.
$$\begin{array}{r} 15 \\ +\ 5 \\ \hline \end{array}$$

3.
$$\begin{array}{r} 9 \\ +\ 5 \\ \hline \end{array}$$

4.
$$\begin{array}{r} 11 \\ +\ 5 \\ \hline \end{array}$$

5.
$$\begin{array}{r} 17 \\ +\ 5 \\ \hline \end{array}$$

6.
$$\begin{array}{r} 5 \\ +\ 5 \\ \hline \end{array}$$

7.
$$\begin{array}{r} 13 \\ +\ 5 \\ \hline \end{array}$$

8.
$$\begin{array}{r} 8 \\ +\ 5 \\ \hline \end{array}$$

9.
$$\begin{array}{r} 15 \\ +\ 5 \\ \hline \end{array}$$

10.
$$\begin{array}{r} 4 \\ +\ 5 \\ \hline \end{array}$$

11.
$$\begin{array}{r} 6 \\ +\ 5 \\ \hline \end{array}$$

12.
$$\begin{array}{r} 1 \\ +\ 5 \\ \hline \end{array}$$

13.
$$\begin{array}{r} 18 \\ +\ 5 \\ \hline \end{array}$$

14.
$$\begin{array}{r} 14 \\ +\ 5 \\ \hline \end{array}$$

15.
$$\begin{array}{r} 19 \\ +\ 5 \\ \hline \end{array}$$

16.
$$\begin{array}{r} 16 \\ +\ 5 \\ \hline \end{array}$$

17.
$$\begin{array}{r} 10 \\ +\ 5 \\ \hline \end{array}$$

18.
$$\begin{array}{r} 3 \\ +\ 5 \\ \hline \end{array}$$

19.
$$\begin{array}{r} 7 \\ +\ 5 \\ \hline \end{array}$$

20.
$$\begin{array}{r} 20 \\ +\ 5 \\ \hline \end{array}$$

IF87115 *Timed Math Tests*

Addition Practice

Name _____ Date _____

Time _____ Score _____

🕐 My time goal is _____ .

1. $\begin{array}{r} 5 \\ + 2 \\ \hline \end{array}$

2. $\begin{array}{r} 5 \\ + 17 \\ \hline \end{array}$

3. $\begin{array}{r} 5 \\ + 13 \\ \hline \end{array}$

4. $\begin{array}{r} 5 \\ + 10 \\ \hline \end{array}$

5. $\begin{array}{r} 5 \\ + 6 \\ \hline \end{array}$

6. $\begin{array}{r} 5 \\ + 19 \\ \hline \end{array}$

7. $\begin{array}{r} 5 \\ + 14 \\ \hline \end{array}$

8. $\begin{array}{r} 5 \\ + 8 \\ \hline \end{array}$

9. $\begin{array}{r} 5 \\ + 1 \\ \hline \end{array}$

10. $\begin{array}{r} 5 \\ + 16 \\ \hline \end{array}$

11. $\begin{array}{r} 5 \\ + 4 \\ \hline \end{array}$

12. $\begin{array}{r} 5 \\ + 12 \\ \hline \end{array}$

13. $\begin{array}{r} 5 \\ + 18 \\ \hline \end{array}$

14. $\begin{array}{r} 5 \\ + 3 \\ \hline \end{array}$

15. $\begin{array}{r} 5 \\ + 15 \\ \hline \end{array}$

16. $\begin{array}{r} 5 \\ + 7 \\ \hline \end{array}$

17. $\begin{array}{r} 5 \\ + 11 \\ \hline \end{array}$

18. $\begin{array}{r} 5 \\ + 9 \\ \hline \end{array}$

19. $\begin{array}{r} 5 \\ + 5 \\ \hline \end{array}$

20. $\begin{array}{r} 5 \\ + 20 \\ \hline \end{array}$

IF87115 *Timed Math Tests*

Addition Challenge

+5C

Name _____ Date _____

Time _____ Score _____

My time goal is _____ .

1.
□
+ 5
11

2.
□
+ 5
14

3.
□
+ 5
20

4.
□
+ 5
16

5.
□
+ 5
21

6.
□
+ 5
24

7.
□
+ 5
6

8.
□
+ 5
22

9.
□
+ 5
8

10.
□
+ 5
18

11.
□
+ 5
10

12.
□
+ 5
12

13.
□
+ 5
23

14.
□
+ 5
15

15.
□
+ 5
9

16.
□
+ 5
7

17.
□
+ 5
19

18.
□
+ 5
25

19.
□
+ 5
13

20.
□
+ 5
17

IF87115 *Timed Math Tests*

Addition Pretest

Name _____   Date _____

Time _____   Score _____

My time goal is _____ .

1. 20
   + 6

2. 5
   + 6

3. 9
   + 6

4. 11
   + 6

5. 7
   + 6

6. 15
   + 6

7. 3
   + 6

8. 18
   + 6

9. 12
   + 6

10. 4
   + 6

11. 16
   + 6

12. 1
   + 6

13. 8
   + 6

14. 14
   + 6

15. 19
   + 6

16. 6
   + 6

17. 10
   + 6

18. 13
   + 6

19. 17
   + 6

20. 2
   + 6

IF87115 *Timed Math Tests*

Addition Practice

Name _____ Date _____

Time _____ Score _____

🕐 My time goal is _____ .

1.
$$\begin{array}{r} 6 \\ +\ 2 \\ \hline \end{array}$$

2.
$$\begin{array}{r} 6 \\ +\ 17 \\ \hline \end{array}$$

3.
$$\begin{array}{r} 6 \\ +\ 13 \\ \hline \end{array}$$

4.
$$\begin{array}{r} 6 \\ +\ 10 \\ \hline \end{array}$$

5.
$$\begin{array}{r} 6 \\ +\ 6 \\ \hline \end{array}$$

6.
$$\begin{array}{r} 6 \\ +\ 19 \\ \hline \end{array}$$

7.
$$\begin{array}{r} 6 \\ +\ 14 \\ \hline \end{array}$$

8.
$$\begin{array}{r} 6 \\ +\ 8 \\ \hline \end{array}$$

9.
$$\begin{array}{r} 6 \\ +\ 1 \\ \hline \end{array}$$

10.
$$\begin{array}{r} 6 \\ +\ 16 \\ \hline \end{array}$$

11.
$$\begin{array}{r} 6 \\ +\ 4 \\ \hline \end{array}$$

12.
$$\begin{array}{r} 6 \\ +\ 12 \\ \hline \end{array}$$

13.
$$\begin{array}{r} 6 \\ +\ 18 \\ \hline \end{array}$$

14.
$$\begin{array}{r} 6 \\ +\ 3 \\ \hline \end{array}$$

15.
$$\begin{array}{r} 6 \\ +\ 15 \\ \hline \end{array}$$

16.
$$\begin{array}{r} 6 \\ +\ 7 \\ \hline \end{array}$$

17.
$$\begin{array}{r} 6 \\ +\ 11 \\ \hline \end{array}$$

18.
$$\begin{array}{r} 6 \\ +\ 9 \\ \hline \end{array}$$

19.
$$\begin{array}{r} 6 \\ +\ 5 \\ \hline \end{array}$$

20.
$$\begin{array}{r} 6 \\ +\ 20 \\ \hline \end{array}$$

IF87115 *Timed Math Tests*

Addition Challenge

Name _____ Date _____

Time _____ Score _____

My time goal is _____ .

1.
$$\begin{array}{r} \square \\ +\ 6 \\ \hline 21 \end{array}$$

2.
$$\begin{array}{r} \square \\ +\ 6 \\ \hline 14 \end{array}$$

3.
$$\begin{array}{r} \square \\ +\ 6 \\ \hline 10 \end{array}$$

4.
$$\begin{array}{r} \square \\ +\ 6 \\ \hline 6 \end{array}$$

5.
$$\begin{array}{r} \square \\ +\ 6 \\ \hline 12 \end{array}$$

6.
$$\begin{array}{r} \square \\ +\ 6 \\ \hline 24 \end{array}$$

7.
$$\begin{array}{r} \square \\ +\ 6 \\ \hline 16 \end{array}$$

8.
$$\begin{array}{r} \square \\ +\ 6 \\ \hline 22 \end{array}$$

9.
$$\begin{array}{r} \square \\ +\ 6 \\ \hline 8 \end{array}$$

10.
$$\begin{array}{r} \square \\ +\ 6 \\ \hline 18 \end{array}$$

11.
$$\begin{array}{r} \square \\ +\ 6 \\ \hline 20 \end{array}$$

12.
$$\begin{array}{r} \square \\ +\ 6 \\ \hline 11 \end{array}$$

13.
$$\begin{array}{r} \square \\ +\ 6 \\ \hline 23 \end{array}$$

14.
$$\begin{array}{r} \square \\ +\ 6 \\ \hline 15 \end{array}$$

15.
$$\begin{array}{r} \square \\ +\ 6 \\ \hline 9 \end{array}$$

16.
$$\begin{array}{r} \square \\ +\ 6 \\ \hline 7 \end{array}$$

17.
$$\begin{array}{r} \square \\ +\ 6 \\ \hline 19 \end{array}$$

18.
$$\begin{array}{r} \square \\ +\ 6 \\ \hline 25 \end{array}$$

19.
$$\begin{array}{r} \square \\ +\ 6 \\ \hline 13 \end{array}$$

20.
$$\begin{array}{r} \square \\ +\ 6 \\ \hline 17 \end{array}$$

IF87115 *Timed Math Tests*

+7A

Name _____ Date _____

Time _____ Score _____

🕭 My time goal is _____ .

1.	2.	3.	4.	5.
2 + 7	15 + 7	9 + 7	11 + 7	17 + 7

6.	7.	8.	9.	10.
5 + 7	13 + 7	8 + 7	12 + 7	4 + 7

11.	12.	13.	14.	15.
6 + 7	1 + 7	18 + 7	17 + 7	19 + 7

16.	17.	18.	19.	20.
16 + 7	10 + 7	3 + 7	7 + 7	20 + 7

IF87115 *Timed Math Tests*

Addition Practice

Name _____   Date _____

Time _____   Score _____

🕐 My time goal is _____ .

1. 7
    + 2

2. 7
    + 17

3. 7
    + 13

4. 7
    + 10

5. 7
    + 6

6. 7
    + 19

7. 7
    + 14

8. 7
    + 8

9. 7
    + 1

10. 7
    + 16

11. 7
    + 4

12. 7
    + 12

13. 7
    + 18

14. 7
    + 3

15. 7
    + 15

16. 7
    + 7

17. 7
    + 11

18. 7
    + 9

19. 7
    + 5

20. 7
    + 20

IF87115 *Timed Math Tests*

Addition Challenge

Name _____   Date _____

Time _____   Score _____

My time goal is _____ .

1.
$$\begin{array}{r} \square \\ +\ 7 \\ \hline 11 \end{array}$$

2.
$$\begin{array}{r} \square \\ +\ 7 \\ \hline 14 \end{array}$$

3.
$$\begin{array}{r} \square \\ +\ 7 \\ \hline 20 \end{array}$$

4.
$$\begin{array}{r} \square \\ +\ 7 \\ \hline 16 \end{array}$$

5.
$$\begin{array}{r} \square \\ +\ 7 \\ \hline 21 \end{array}$$

6.
$$\begin{array}{r} \square \\ +\ 7 \\ \hline 24 \end{array}$$

7.
$$\begin{array}{r} \square \\ +\ 7 \\ \hline 26 \end{array}$$

8.
$$\begin{array}{r} \square \\ +\ 7 \\ \hline 22 \end{array}$$

9.
$$\begin{array}{r} \square \\ +\ 7 \\ \hline 8 \end{array}$$

10.
$$\begin{array}{r} \square \\ +\ 7 \\ \hline 18 \end{array}$$

11.
$$\begin{array}{r} \square \\ +\ 7 \\ \hline 10 \end{array}$$

12.
$$\begin{array}{r} \square \\ +\ 7 \\ \hline 12 \end{array}$$

13.
$$\begin{array}{r} \square \\ +\ 7 \\ \hline 23 \end{array}$$

14.
$$\begin{array}{r} \square \\ +\ 7 \\ \hline 15 \end{array}$$

15.
$$\begin{array}{r} \square \\ +\ 7 \\ \hline 9 \end{array}$$

16.
$$\begin{array}{r} \square \\ +\ 7 \\ \hline 27 \end{array}$$

17.
$$\begin{array}{r} \square \\ +\ 7 \\ \hline 19 \end{array}$$

18.
$$\begin{array}{r} \square \\ +\ 7 \\ \hline 25 \end{array}$$

19.
$$\begin{array}{r} \square \\ +\ 7 \\ \hline 13 \end{array}$$

20.
$$\begin{array}{r} \square \\ +\ 7 \\ \hline 17 \end{array}$$

IF87115 Timed Math Tests

Addition Pretest

Name _____   Date _____

Time _____   Score _____

🕐 My time goal is _____ .

1. 20
   + 8

2.   5
   + 8

3.   9
   + 8

4. 11
   + 8

5.   7
   + 8

6. 15
   + 8

7.   3
   + 8

8. 18
   + 8

9. 12
   + 8

10. 4
   + 8

11. 16
   + 8

12. 1
   + 8

13. 8
   + 8

14. 14
   + 8

15. 19
   + 8

16. 6
   + 8

17. 10
   + 8

18. 13
   + 8

19. 17
   + 8

20. 2
   + 8

IF87115 *Timed Math Tests*

Addition Practice

Name _____   Date _____

Time _____   Score _____

My time goal is _____ .

1.
$$8$$
$$+\ 2$$

2.
$$8$$
$$+\ 17$$

3.
$$8$$
$$+\ 13$$

4.
$$8$$
$$+\ 10$$

5.
$$8$$
$$+\ 6$$

6.
$$8$$
$$+\ 19$$

7.
$$8$$
$$+\ 14$$

8.
$$8$$
$$+\ 8$$

9.
$$8$$
$$+\ 1$$

10.
$$8$$
$$+\ 16$$

11.
$$8$$
$$+\ 4$$

12.
$$8$$
$$+\ 12$$

13.
$$8$$
$$+\ 18$$

14.
$$8$$
$$+\ 3$$

15.
$$8$$
$$+\ 15$$

16.
$$8$$
$$+\ 7$$

17.
$$8$$
$$+\ 11$$

18.
$$8$$
$$+\ 9$$

19.
$$8$$
$$+\ 5$$

20.
$$8$$
$$+\ 20$$

Addition Challenge

Name _____   Date _____

Time _____   Score _____

🕐 My time goal is _____ .

1.
$$\square + 8 = 21$$

2.
$$\square + 8 = 14$$

3.
$$\square + 8 = 10$$

4.
$$\square + 8 = 26$$

5.
$$\square + 8 = 12$$

6.
$$\square + 8 = 24$$

7.
$$\square + 8 = 16$$

8.
$$\square + 8 = 22$$

9.
$$\square + 8 = 8$$

10.
$$\square + 8 = 18$$

11.
$$\square + 8 = 20$$

12.
$$\square + 8 = 11$$

13.
$$\square + 8 = 23$$

14.
$$\square + 8 = 15$$

15.
$$\square + 8 = 9$$

16.
$$\square + 8 = 27$$

17.
$$\square + 8 = 19$$

18.
$$\square + 8 = 25$$

19.
$$\square + 8 = 13$$

20.
$$\square + 8 = 17$$

IF87115 *Timed Math Tests*

Addition Pretest

Name _____ Date _____

Time _____ Score _____

My time goal is _____ .

1.
$$\begin{array}{r} 2 \\ +\ 9 \\ \hline \end{array}$$

2.
$$\begin{array}{r} 15 \\ +\ 9 \\ \hline \end{array}$$

3.
$$\begin{array}{r} 9 \\ +\ 9 \\ \hline \end{array}$$

4.
$$\begin{array}{r} 11 \\ +\ 9 \\ \hline \end{array}$$

5.
$$\begin{array}{r} 17 \\ +\ 9 \\ \hline \end{array}$$

6.
$$\begin{array}{r} 5 \\ +\ 9 \\ \hline \end{array}$$

7.
$$\begin{array}{r} 13 \\ +\ 9 \\ \hline \end{array}$$

8.
$$\begin{array}{r} 8 \\ +\ 9 \\ \hline \end{array}$$

9.
$$\begin{array}{r} 12 \\ +\ 9 \\ \hline \end{array}$$

10.
$$\begin{array}{r} 4 \\ +\ 9 \\ \hline \end{array}$$

11.
$$\begin{array}{r} 6 \\ +\ 9 \\ \hline \end{array}$$

12.
$$\begin{array}{r} 1 \\ +\ 9 \\ \hline \end{array}$$

13.
$$\begin{array}{r} 18 \\ +\ 9 \\ \hline \end{array}$$

14.
$$\begin{array}{r} 14 \\ +\ 9 \\ \hline \end{array}$$

15.
$$\begin{array}{r} 19 \\ +\ 9 \\ \hline \end{array}$$

16.
$$\begin{array}{r} 16 \\ +\ 9 \\ \hline \end{array}$$

17.
$$\begin{array}{r} 10 \\ +\ 9 \\ \hline \end{array}$$

18.
$$\begin{array}{r} 3 \\ +\ 9 \\ \hline \end{array}$$

19.
$$\begin{array}{r} 7 \\ +\ 9 \\ \hline \end{array}$$

20.
$$\begin{array}{r} 20 \\ +\ 9 \\ \hline \end{array}$$

IF87115 *Timed Math Tests*

Addition Practice

Name _____ Date _____

Time _____ Score _____

My time goal is _____ .

1. 9
    + 2

2. 9
    + 17

3. 9
    + 13

4. 9
    + 10

5. 9
    + 6

6. 9
    + 19

7. 9
    + 14

8. 9
    + 8

9. 9
    + 1

10. 9
    + 16

11. 9
    + 4

12. 9
    + 12

13. 9
    + 18

14. 9
    + 3

15. 9
    + 15

16. 9
    + 7

17. 9
    + 11

18. 9
    + 9

19. 9
    + 5

20. 9
    + 20

IF87115 *Timed Math Tests*

Addition Challenge

Name _____   Date _____

Time _____   Score _____

🕐 My time goal is _____ .

1.
$$\begin{array}{r} \square \\ +\ 9 \\ \hline 11 \end{array}$$

2.
$$\begin{array}{r} \square \\ +\ 9 \\ \hline 14 \end{array}$$

3.
$$\begin{array}{r} \square \\ +\ 9 \\ \hline 20 \end{array}$$

4.
$$\begin{array}{r} \square \\ +\ 9 \\ \hline 16 \end{array}$$

5.
$$\begin{array}{r} \square \\ +\ 9 \\ \hline 21 \end{array}$$

6.
$$\begin{array}{r} \square \\ +\ 9 \\ \hline 24 \end{array}$$

7.
$$\begin{array}{r} \square \\ +\ 9 \\ \hline 26 \end{array}$$

8.
$$\begin{array}{r} \square \\ +\ 9 \\ \hline 22 \end{array}$$

9.
$$\begin{array}{r} \square \\ +\ 9 \\ \hline 25 \end{array}$$

10.
$$\begin{array}{r} \square \\ +\ 9 \\ \hline 18 \end{array}$$

11.
$$\begin{array}{r} \square \\ +\ 9 \\ \hline 10 \end{array}$$

12.
$$\begin{array}{r} \square \\ +\ 9 \\ \hline 12 \end{array}$$

13.
$$\begin{array}{r} \square \\ +\ 9 \\ \hline 23 \end{array}$$

14.
$$\begin{array}{r} \square \\ +\ 9 \\ \hline 15 \end{array}$$

15.
$$\begin{array}{r} \square \\ +\ 9 \\ \hline 9 \end{array}$$

16.
$$\begin{array}{r} \square \\ +\ 9 \\ \hline 27 \end{array}$$

17.
$$\begin{array}{r} \square \\ +\ 9 \\ \hline 19 \end{array}$$

18.
$$\begin{array}{r} \square \\ +\ 9 \\ \hline 25 \end{array}$$

19.
$$\begin{array}{r} \square \\ +\ 9 \\ \hline 13 \end{array}$$

20.
$$\begin{array}{r} \square \\ +\ 9 \\ \hline 17 \end{array}$$

IF87115 *Timed Math Tests*

Addition Pretest

Name _____ Date _____

Time _____ Score _____

🕐 My time goal is _____ .

1. $\begin{array}{r} 9 \\ +10 \\ \hline \end{array}$	2. $\begin{array}{r} 19 \\ +10 \\ \hline \end{array}$	3. $\begin{array}{r} 4 \\ +10 \\ \hline \end{array}$	4. $\begin{array}{r} 6 \\ +10 \\ \hline \end{array}$	5. $\begin{array}{r} 2 \\ +10 \\ \hline \end{array}$
6. $\begin{array}{r} 8 \\ +10 \\ \hline \end{array}$	7. $\begin{array}{r} 10 \\ +10 \\ \hline \end{array}$	8. $\begin{array}{r} 16 \\ +10 \\ \hline \end{array}$	9. $\begin{array}{r} 5 \\ +10 \\ \hline \end{array}$	10. $\begin{array}{r} 14 \\ +10 \\ \hline \end{array}$
11. $\begin{array}{r} 7 \\ +10 \\ \hline \end{array}$	12. $\begin{array}{r} 20 \\ +10 \\ \hline \end{array}$	13. $\begin{array}{r} 15 \\ +10 \\ \hline \end{array}$	14. $\begin{array}{r} 12 \\ +10 \\ \hline \end{array}$	15. $\begin{array}{r} 18 \\ +10 \\ \hline \end{array}$
16. $\begin{array}{r} 3 \\ +10 \\ \hline \end{array}$	17. $\begin{array}{r} 17 \\ +10 \\ \hline \end{array}$	18. $\begin{array}{r} 11 \\ +10 \\ \hline \end{array}$	19. $\begin{array}{r} 13 \\ +10 \\ \hline \end{array}$	20. $\begin{array}{r} 1 \\ +10 \\ \hline \end{array}$

Addition Practice

Name _____   Date _____

Time _____   Score _____

🕐 My time goal is _____ .

1. 10 + 7	2. 10 + 17	3. 10 + 20	4. 10 + 15	5. 10 + 12
6. 10 + 18	7. 10 + 3	8. 10 + 1	9. 10 + 11	10. 10 + 13
11. 10 + 14	12. 10 + 5	13. 10 + 16	14. 10 + 10	15. 10 + 8
16. 10 + 2	17. 10 + 6	18. 10 + 4	19. 10 + 19	20. 10 + 9

IF87115 *Timed Math Tests*

Addition Challenge

Name _____   Date _____

Time _____   Score _____

⏰ My time goal is _____ .

1.
$$\begin{array}{r} \square \\ +\ 10 \\ \hline 21 \end{array}$$

2.
$$\begin{array}{r} \square \\ +\ 10 \\ \hline 19 \end{array}$$

3.
$$\begin{array}{r} \square \\ +\ 10 \\ \hline 12 \end{array}$$

4.
$$\begin{array}{r} \square \\ +\ 10 \\ \hline 23 \end{array}$$

5.
$$\begin{array}{r} \square \\ +\ 10 \\ \hline 15 \end{array}$$

6.
$$\begin{array}{r} \square \\ +\ 10 \\ \hline 25 \end{array}$$

7.
$$\begin{array}{r} \square \\ +\ 10 \\ \hline 11 \end{array}$$

8.
$$\begin{array}{r} \square \\ +\ 10 \\ \hline 22 \end{array}$$

9.
$$\begin{array}{r} \square \\ +\ 10 \\ \hline 20 \end{array}$$

10.
$$\begin{array}{r} \square \\ +\ 10 \\ \hline 26 \end{array}$$

11.
$$\begin{array}{r} \square \\ +\ 10 \\ \hline 18 \end{array}$$

12.
$$\begin{array}{r} \square \\ +\ 10 \\ \hline 24 \end{array}$$

13.
$$\begin{array}{r} \square \\ +\ 10 \\ \hline 29 \end{array}$$

14.
$$\begin{array}{r} \square \\ +\ 10 \\ \hline 13 \end{array}$$

15.
$$\begin{array}{r} \square \\ +\ 10 \\ \hline 10 \end{array}$$

16.
$$\begin{array}{r} \square \\ +\ 10 \\ \hline 16 \end{array}$$

17.
$$\begin{array}{r} \square \\ +\ 10 \\ \hline 27 \end{array}$$

18.
$$\begin{array}{r} \square \\ +\ 10 \\ \hline 17 \end{array}$$

19.
$$\begin{array}{r} \square \\ +\ 10 \\ \hline 28 \end{array}$$

20.
$$\begin{array}{r} \square \\ +\ 10 \\ \hline 14 \end{array}$$

IF87115 *Timed Math Tests*

Addition Pretest

Name _____   Date _____

Time _____   Score _____

🕐 My time goal is _____ .

1.
$$\begin{array}{r} 20 \\ +11 \\ \hline \end{array}$$

2.
$$\begin{array}{r} 5 \\ +11 \\ \hline \end{array}$$

3.
$$\begin{array}{r} 9 \\ +11 \\ \hline \end{array}$$

4.
$$\begin{array}{r} 11 \\ +11 \\ \hline \end{array}$$

5.
$$\begin{array}{r} 7 \\ +11 \\ \hline \end{array}$$

6.
$$\begin{array}{r} 15 \\ +11 \\ \hline \end{array}$$

7.
$$\begin{array}{r} 3 \\ +11 \\ \hline \end{array}$$

8.
$$\begin{array}{r} 18 \\ +11 \\ \hline \end{array}$$

9.
$$\begin{array}{r} 12 \\ +11 \\ \hline \end{array}$$

10.
$$\begin{array}{r} 4 \\ +11 \\ \hline \end{array}$$

11.
$$\begin{array}{r} 16 \\ +11 \\ \hline \end{array}$$

12.
$$\begin{array}{r} 1 \\ +11 \\ \hline \end{array}$$

13.
$$\begin{array}{r} 8 \\ +11 \\ \hline \end{array}$$

14.
$$\begin{array}{r} 14 \\ +11 \\ \hline \end{array}$$

15.
$$\begin{array}{r} 19 \\ +11 \\ \hline \end{array}$$

16.
$$\begin{array}{r} 6 \\ +11 \\ \hline \end{array}$$

17.
$$\begin{array}{r} 10 \\ +11 \\ \hline \end{array}$$

18.
$$\begin{array}{r} 13 \\ +11 \\ \hline \end{array}$$

19.
$$\begin{array}{r} 17 \\ +11 \\ \hline \end{array}$$

20.
$$\begin{array}{r} 2 \\ +11 \\ \hline \end{array}$$

Addition Practice

Name _____   Date _____

Time _____   Score _____

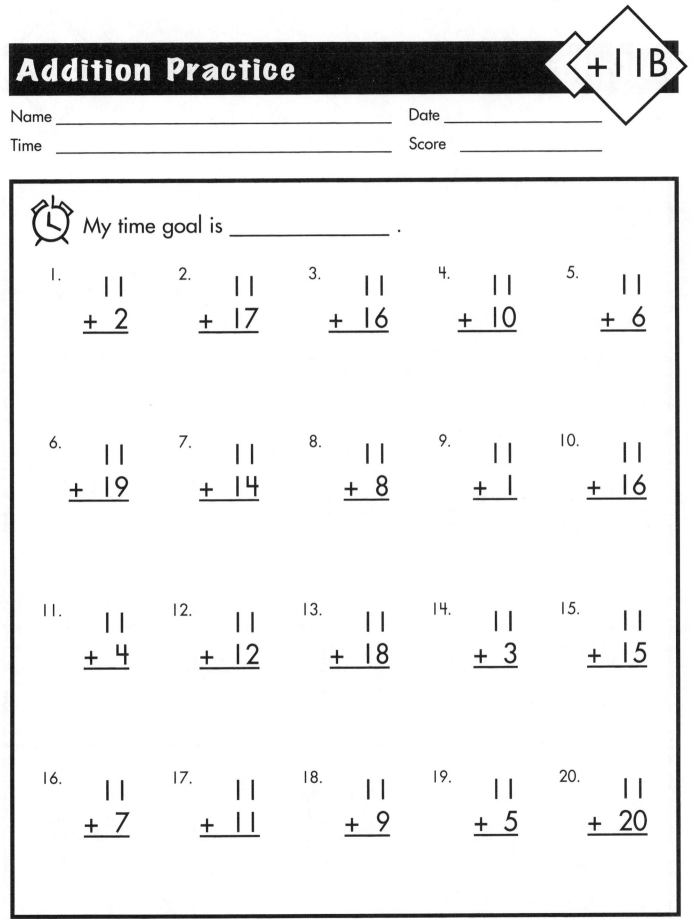

My time goal is _____ .

1. 11
    + 2

2. 11
    + 17

3. 11
    + 16

4. 11
    + 10

5. 11
    + 6

6. 11
    + 19

7. 11
    + 14

8. 11
    + 8

9. 11
    + 1

10. 11
    + 16

11. 11
    + 4

12. 11
    + 12

13. 11
    + 18

14. 11
    + 3

15. 11
    + 15

16. 11
    + 7

17. 11
    + 11

18. 11
    + 9

19. 11
    + 5

20. 11
    + 20

IF87115 *Timed Math Tests*

Addition Challenge

+11C

Name _____   Date _____

Time _____   Score _____

🕐 My time goal is _____ .

1.
$$\square + 11 \over 21$$

2.
$$\square + 11 \over 14$$

3.
$$\square + 11 \over 12$$

4.
$$\square + 11 \over 25$$

5.
$$\square + 11 \over 24$$

6.
$$\square + 11 \over 16$$

7.
$$\square + 11 \over 22$$

8.
$$\square + 11 \over 28$$

9.
$$\square + 11 \over 18$$

10.
$$\square + 11 \over 26$$

11.
$$\square + 11 \over 20$$

12.
$$\square + 11 \over 11$$

13.
$$\square + 11 \over 23$$

14.
$$\square + 11 \over 15$$

15.
$$\square + 11 \over 30$$

16.
$$\square + 11 \over 27$$

17.
$$\square + 11 \over 19$$

18.
$$\square + 11 \over 29$$

19.
$$\square + 11 \over 13$$

20.
$$\square + 11 \over 17$$

IF87115 *Timed Math Tests*

Addition Pretest

Name _____ Date _____

Time _____ Score _____

My time goal is _____ .

1.
$$\begin{array}{r} 6 \\ + 12 \\ \hline \end{array}$$

2.
$$\begin{array}{r} 1 \\ + 12 \\ \hline \end{array}$$

3.
$$\begin{array}{r} 18 \\ + 12 \\ \hline \end{array}$$

4.
$$\begin{array}{r} 14 \\ + 12 \\ \hline \end{array}$$

5.
$$\begin{array}{r} 19 \\ + 12 \\ \hline \end{array}$$

6.
$$\begin{array}{r} 16 \\ + 12 \\ \hline \end{array}$$

7.
$$\begin{array}{r} 10 \\ + 12 \\ \hline \end{array}$$

8.
$$\begin{array}{r} 3 \\ + 12 \\ \hline \end{array}$$

9.
$$\begin{array}{r} 7 \\ + 12 \\ \hline \end{array}$$

10.
$$\begin{array}{r} 20 \\ + 12 \\ \hline \end{array}$$

11.
$$\begin{array}{r} 4 \\ + 12 \\ \hline \end{array}$$

12.
$$\begin{array}{r} 12 \\ + 12 \\ \hline \end{array}$$

13.
$$\begin{array}{r} 8 \\ + 12 \\ \hline \end{array}$$

14.
$$\begin{array}{r} 13 \\ + 12 \\ \hline \end{array}$$

15.
$$\begin{array}{r} 5 \\ + 12 \\ \hline \end{array}$$

16.
$$\begin{array}{r} 17 \\ + 12 \\ \hline \end{array}$$

17.
$$\begin{array}{r} 11 \\ + 12 \\ \hline \end{array}$$

18.
$$\begin{array}{r} 9 \\ + 12 \\ \hline \end{array}$$

19.
$$\begin{array}{r} 15 \\ + 12 \\ \hline \end{array}$$

20.
$$\begin{array}{r} 2 \\ + 12 \\ \hline \end{array}$$

Addition Practice

Name _____ Date _____

Time _____ Score _____

My time goal is _____ .

1.	2.	3.	4.	5.
12 + 2	12 + 17	12 + 13	12 + 10	12 + 11

6.	7.	8.	9.	10.
12 + 6	12 + 19	12 + 14	12 + 8	12 + 1

11.	12.	13.	14.	15.
12 + 16	12 + 4	12 + 12	12 + 18	12 + 3

16.	17.	18.	19.	20.
12 + 15	12 + 7	12 + 9	12 + 5	12 + 20

IF87115 *Timed Math Tests*

Addition Challenge

Name _____ Date _____

Time _____ Score _____

🕐 My time goal is _____ .

1. $\square$
    $+ 12$
    $\overline{12}$

2. $\square$
    $+ 12$
    $\overline{14}$

3. $\square$
    $+ 12$
    $\overline{20}$

4. $\square$
    $+ 12$
    $\overline{16}$

5. $\square$
    $+ 12$
    $\overline{21}$

6. $\square$
    $+ 12$
    $\overline{24}$

7. $\square$
    $+ 12$
    $\overline{16}$

8. $\square$
    $+ 12$
    $\overline{22}$

9. $\square$
    $+ 12$
    $\overline{28}$

10. $\square$
    $+ 12$
    $\overline{18}$

11. $\square$
    $+ 12$
    $\overline{30}$

12. $\square$
    $+ 12$
    $\overline{23}$

13. $\square$
    $+ 12$
    $\overline{15}$

14. $\square$
    $+ 12$
    $\overline{29}$

15. $\square$
    $+ 12$
    $\overline{27}$

16. $\square$
    $+ 12$
    $\overline{19}$

17. $\square$
    $+ 12$
    $\overline{25}$

18. $\square$
    $+ 12$
    $\overline{13}$

19. $\square$
    $+ 12$
    $\overline{17}$

20. $\square$
    $+ 12$
    $\overline{31}$

IF87115 *Timed Math Tests*

Addition Pretest

Name _____   Date _____

Time _____   Score _____

🕐 My time goal is _____ .

1. 20
   + 13

2.   5
   + 13

3.   9
   + 13

4. 11
   + 13

5.   7
   + 13

6. 15
   + 13

7.   3
   + 13

8. 18
   + 13

9. 12
   + 13

10. 4
   + 13

11. 16
   + 13

12.   1
   + 13

13.   8
   + 13

14. 14
   + 13

15. 19
   + 13

16.   6
   + 13

17. 10
   + 13

18. 13
   + 13

19. 17
   + 13

20.   2
   + 13

Addition Practice

Name _____   Date _____

Time _____   Score _____

🕐 My time goal is _____ .

1.
$$\begin{array}{r} 13 \\ +\ 2 \\ \hline \end{array}$$

2.
$$\begin{array}{r} 13 \\ +\ 17 \\ \hline \end{array}$$

3.
$$\begin{array}{r} 13 \\ +\ 13 \\ \hline \end{array}$$

4.
$$\begin{array}{r} 13 \\ +\ 10 \\ \hline \end{array}$$

5.
$$\begin{array}{r} 13 \\ +\ 6 \\ \hline \end{array}$$

6.
$$\begin{array}{r} 13 \\ +\ 19 \\ \hline \end{array}$$

7.
$$\begin{array}{r} 13 \\ +\ 14 \\ \hline \end{array}$$

8.
$$\begin{array}{r} 13 \\ +\ 8 \\ \hline \end{array}$$

9.
$$\begin{array}{r} 13 \\ +\ 1 \\ \hline \end{array}$$

10.
$$\begin{array}{r} 13 \\ +\ 16 \\ \hline \end{array}$$

11.
$$\begin{array}{r} 13 \\ +\ 4 \\ \hline \end{array}$$

12.
$$\begin{array}{r} 13 \\ +\ 12 \\ \hline \end{array}$$

13.
$$\begin{array}{r} 13 \\ +\ 18 \\ \hline \end{array}$$

14.
$$\begin{array}{r} 13 \\ +\ 3 \\ \hline \end{array}$$

15.
$$\begin{array}{r} 13 \\ +\ 15 \\ \hline \end{array}$$

16.
$$\begin{array}{r} 13 \\ +\ 7 \\ \hline \end{array}$$

17.
$$\begin{array}{r} 13 \\ +\ 11 \\ \hline \end{array}$$

18.
$$\begin{array}{r} 13 \\ +\ 9 \\ \hline \end{array}$$

19.
$$\begin{array}{r} 13 \\ +\ 5 \\ \hline \end{array}$$

20.
$$\begin{array}{r} 13 \\ +\ 20 \\ \hline \end{array}$$

IF87115 *Timed Math Tests*

Addition Challenge

Name _____ Date _____

Time _____ Score _____

🕐 My time goal is _____ .

1. ☐
   + 13
   ____
    21

2. ☐
   + 13
   ____
    14

3. ☐
   + 13
   ____
    31

4. ☐
   + 13
   ____
    26

5. ☐
   + 13
   ____
    13

6. ☐
   + 13
   ____
    24

7. ☐
   + 13
   ____
    16

8. ☐
   + 13
   ____
    22

9. ☐
   + 13
   ____
    28

10. ☐
   + 13
   ____
    18

11. ☐
   + 13
   ____
    20

12. ☐
   + 13
   ____
    30

13. ☐
   + 13
   ____
    23

14. ☐
   + 13
   ____
    15

15. ☐
   + 13
   ____
    29

16. ☐
   + 13
   ____
    19

17. ☐
   + 13
   ____
    27

18. ☐
   + 13
   ____
    25

19. ☐
   + 13
   ____
    13

20. ☐
   + 13
   ____
    17

IF87115 *Timed Math Tests*

Addition Pretest

Name _____ Date _____

Time _____ Score _____

My time goal is _____ .

1.
$$\begin{array}{r} 2 \\ +\ 14 \\ \hline \end{array}$$

2.
$$\begin{array}{r} 15 \\ +\ 14 \\ \hline \end{array}$$

3.
$$\begin{array}{r} 9 \\ +\ 14 \\ \hline \end{array}$$

4.
$$\begin{array}{r} 11 \\ +\ 14 \\ \hline \end{array}$$

5.
$$\begin{array}{r} 17 \\ +\ 14 \\ \hline \end{array}$$

6.
$$\begin{array}{r} 5 \\ +\ 14 \\ \hline \end{array}$$

7.
$$\begin{array}{r} 13 \\ +\ 14 \\ \hline \end{array}$$

8.
$$\begin{array}{r} 8 \\ +\ 14 \\ \hline \end{array}$$

9.
$$\begin{array}{r} 12 \\ +\ 14 \\ \hline \end{array}$$

10.
$$\begin{array}{r} 4 \\ +\ 14 \\ \hline \end{array}$$

11.
$$\begin{array}{r} 6 \\ +\ 14 \\ \hline \end{array}$$

12.
$$\begin{array}{r} 1 \\ +\ 14 \\ \hline \end{array}$$

13.
$$\begin{array}{r} 18 \\ +\ 14 \\ \hline \end{array}$$

14.
$$\begin{array}{r} 14 \\ +\ 14 \\ \hline \end{array}$$

15.
$$\begin{array}{r} 19 \\ +\ 14 \\ \hline \end{array}$$

16.
$$\begin{array}{r} 16 \\ +\ 14 \\ \hline \end{array}$$

17.
$$\begin{array}{r} 10 \\ +\ 14 \\ \hline \end{array}$$

18.
$$\begin{array}{r} 3 \\ +\ 14 \\ \hline \end{array}$$

19.
$$\begin{array}{r} 7 \\ +\ 14 \\ \hline \end{array}$$

20.
$$\begin{array}{r} 20 \\ +\ 14 \\ \hline \end{array}$$

IF87115 *Timed Math Tests*

Addition Practice

Name _____   Date _____

Time _____   Score _____

🕐 My time goal is _____ .

1.
$$\begin{array}{r} 14 \\ + \ 2 \\ \hline \end{array}$$

2.
$$\begin{array}{r} 14 \\ + 17 \\ \hline \end{array}$$

3.
$$\begin{array}{r} 14 \\ + 13 \\ \hline \end{array}$$

4.
$$\begin{array}{r} 14 \\ + 10 \\ \hline \end{array}$$

5.
$$\begin{array}{r} 14 \\ + \ 6 \\ \hline \end{array}$$

6.
$$\begin{array}{r} 14 \\ + 19 \\ \hline \end{array}$$

7.
$$\begin{array}{r} 14 \\ + 14 \\ \hline \end{array}$$

8.
$$\begin{array}{r} 14 \\ + \ 8 \\ \hline \end{array}$$

9.
$$\begin{array}{r} 14 \\ + \ 1 \\ \hline \end{array}$$

10.
$$\begin{array}{r} 14 \\ + \ 6 \\ \hline \end{array}$$

11.
$$\begin{array}{r} 14 \\ + \ 4 \\ \hline \end{array}$$

12.
$$\begin{array}{r} 14 \\ + 12 \\ \hline \end{array}$$

13.
$$\begin{array}{r} 14 \\ + 18 \\ \hline \end{array}$$

14.
$$\begin{array}{r} 14 \\ + \ 3 \\ \hline \end{array}$$

15.
$$\begin{array}{r} 14 \\ + 15 \\ \hline \end{array}$$

16.
$$\begin{array}{r} 14 \\ + \ 7 \\ \hline \end{array}$$

17.
$$\begin{array}{r} 14 \\ + 11 \\ \hline \end{array}$$

18.
$$\begin{array}{r} 14 \\ + \ 9 \\ \hline \end{array}$$

19.
$$\begin{array}{r} 14 \\ + \ 5 \\ \hline \end{array}$$

20.
$$\begin{array}{r} 14 \\ + 20 \\ \hline \end{array}$$

IF87115 *Timed Math Tests*

Addition Challenge

Name _____   Date _____

Time _____   Score _____

My time goal is _____ .

1.
$$\begin{array}{r} \square \\ +\ 14 \\ \hline 23 \end{array}$$

2.
$$\begin{array}{r} \square \\ +\ 14 \\ \hline 30 \end{array}$$

3.
$$\begin{array}{r} \square \\ +\ 14 \\ \hline 28 \end{array}$$

4.
$$\begin{array}{r} \square \\ +\ 14 \\ \hline 16 \end{array}$$

5.
$$\begin{array}{r} \square \\ +\ 14 \\ \hline 21 \end{array}$$

6.
$$\begin{array}{r} \square \\ +\ 14 \\ \hline 24 \end{array}$$

7.
$$\begin{array}{r} \square \\ +\ 14 \\ \hline 26 \end{array}$$

8.
$$\begin{array}{r} \square \\ +\ 14 \\ \hline 32 \end{array}$$

9.
$$\begin{array}{r} \square \\ +\ 14 \\ \hline 22 \end{array}$$

10.
$$\begin{array}{r} \square \\ +\ 14 \\ \hline 18 \end{array}$$

11.
$$\begin{array}{r} \square \\ +\ 14 \\ \hline 14 \end{array}$$

12.
$$\begin{array}{r} \square \\ +\ 14 \\ \hline 29 \end{array}$$

13.
$$\begin{array}{r} \square \\ +\ 14 \\ \hline 31 \end{array}$$

14.
$$\begin{array}{r} \square \\ +\ 14 \\ \hline 15 \end{array}$$

15.
$$\begin{array}{r} \square \\ +\ 14 \\ \hline 20 \end{array}$$

16.
$$\begin{array}{r} \square \\ +\ 14 \\ \hline 27 \end{array}$$

17.
$$\begin{array}{r} \square \\ +\ 14 \\ \hline 19 \end{array}$$

18.
$$\begin{array}{r} \square \\ +\ 14 \\ \hline 25 \end{array}$$

19.
$$\begin{array}{r} \square \\ +\ 14 \\ \hline 33 \end{array}$$

20.
$$\begin{array}{r} \square \\ +\ 14 \\ \hline 17 \end{array}$$

IF87115 *Timed Math Tests*

Addition Pretest

Name _____ Date _____

Time _____ Score _____

🕐 My time goal is _____ .

1. $\begin{array}{r} 9 \\ +\ 15 \\ \hline \end{array}$	2. $\begin{array}{r} 19 \\ +\ 15 \\ \hline \end{array}$	3. $\begin{array}{r} 4 \\ +\ 15 \\ \hline \end{array}$	4. $\begin{array}{r} 6 \\ +\ 15 \\ \hline \end{array}$	5. $\begin{array}{r} 2 \\ +\ 15 \\ \hline \end{array}$
6. $\begin{array}{r} 8 \\ +\ 15 \\ \hline \end{array}$	7. $\begin{array}{r} 10 \\ +\ 15 \\ \hline \end{array}$	8. $\begin{array}{r} 16 \\ +\ 15 \\ \hline \end{array}$	9. $\begin{array}{r} 5 \\ +\ 15 \\ \hline \end{array}$	10. $\begin{array}{r} 14 \\ +\ 15 \\ \hline \end{array}$
11. $\begin{array}{r} 7 \\ +\ 15 \\ \hline \end{array}$	12. $\begin{array}{r} 20 \\ +\ 15 \\ \hline \end{array}$	13. $\begin{array}{r} 15 \\ +\ 15 \\ \hline \end{array}$	14. $\begin{array}{r} 12 \\ +\ 15 \\ \hline \end{array}$	15. $\begin{array}{r} 18 \\ +\ 15 \\ \hline \end{array}$
16. $\begin{array}{r} 3 \\ +\ 15 \\ \hline \end{array}$	17. $\begin{array}{r} 17 \\ +\ 15 \\ \hline \end{array}$	18. $\begin{array}{r} 11 \\ +\ 15 \\ \hline \end{array}$	19. $\begin{array}{r} 13 \\ +\ 15 \\ \hline \end{array}$	20. $\begin{array}{r} 1 \\ +\ 15 \\ \hline \end{array}$

IF87115 *Timed Math Tests*

Name _____   Date _____

Time _____   Score _____

🕐 My time goal is _____ .

1. 15
   + 7

2. 15
   + 17

3. 15
   + 20

4. 15
   + 15

5. 15
   + 12

6. 15
   + 18

7. 15
   + 3

8. 15
   + 1

9. 15
   + 11

10. 15
    + 13

11. 15
    + 14

12. 15
    + 5

13. 15
    + 16

14. 15
    + 10

15. 15
    + 8

16. 15
    + 2

17. 15
    + 6

18. 15
    + 4

19. 15
    + 19

20. 15
    + 9

IF87115 *Timed Math Tests*

Addition Challenge

Name _____   Date _____

Time _____   Score _____

My time goal is _____ .

1.
$$\begin{array}{r} \square \\ +\ 15 \\ \hline 21 \end{array}$$

2.
$$\begin{array}{r} \square \\ +\ 15 \\ \hline 32 \end{array}$$

3.
$$\begin{array}{r} \square \\ +\ 15 \\ \hline 25 \end{array}$$

4.
$$\begin{array}{r} \square \\ +\ 15 \\ \hline 34 \end{array}$$

5.
$$\begin{array}{r} \square \\ +\ 15 \\ \hline 24 \end{array}$$

6.
$$\begin{array}{r} \square \\ +\ 15 \\ \hline 16 \end{array}$$

7.
$$\begin{array}{r} \square \\ +\ 15 \\ \hline 22 \end{array}$$

8.
$$\begin{array}{r} \square \\ +\ 15 \\ \hline 28 \end{array}$$

9.
$$\begin{array}{r} \square \\ +\ 15 \\ \hline 18 \end{array}$$

10.
$$\begin{array}{r} \square \\ +\ 15 \\ \hline 26 \end{array}$$

11.
$$\begin{array}{r} \square \\ +\ 15 \\ \hline 20 \end{array}$$

12.
$$\begin{array}{r} \square \\ +\ 15 \\ \hline 30 \end{array}$$

13.
$$\begin{array}{r} \square \\ +\ 15 \\ \hline 23 \end{array}$$

14.
$$\begin{array}{r} \square \\ +\ 15 \\ \hline 15 \end{array}$$

15.
$$\begin{array}{r} \square \\ +\ 15 \\ \hline 31 \end{array}$$

16.
$$\begin{array}{r} \square \\ +\ 15 \\ \hline 27 \end{array}$$

17.
$$\begin{array}{r} \square \\ +\ 15 \\ \hline 19 \end{array}$$

18.
$$\begin{array}{r} \square \\ +\ 15 \\ \hline 29 \end{array}$$

19.
$$\begin{array}{r} \square \\ +\ 15 \\ \hline 33 \end{array}$$

20.
$$\begin{array}{r} \square \\ +\ 15 \\ \hline 17 \end{array}$$

Name _____ Date _____

Time _____ Score _____

🕐 My time goal is _____ .

1.	2.	3.	4.	5.
6 + 16	1 + 16	18 + 16	14 + 16	19 + 16

6.	7.	8.	9.	10.
16 + 16	10 + 16	3 + 16	7 + 16	20 + 16

11.	12.	13.	14.	15.
4 + 16	12 + 16	8 + 16	13 + 16	5 + 16

16.	17.	18.	19.	20.
17 + 16	11 + 16	9 + 16	15 + 16	2 + 16

Addition Practice

Name _____ Date _____

Time _____ Score _____

🕐 My time goal is _____ .

1.
$$\begin{array}{r} 16 \\ +2 \\ \hline \end{array}$$

2.
$$\begin{array}{r} 16 \\ +17 \\ \hline \end{array}$$

3.
$$\begin{array}{r} 16 \\ +13 \\ \hline \end{array}$$

4.
$$\begin{array}{r} 16 \\ +10 \\ \hline \end{array}$$

5.
$$\begin{array}{r} 16 \\ +6 \\ \hline \end{array}$$

6.
$$\begin{array}{r} 16 \\ +19 \\ \hline \end{array}$$

7.
$$\begin{array}{r} 16 \\ +14 \\ \hline \end{array}$$

8.
$$\begin{array}{r} 16 \\ +8 \\ \hline \end{array}$$

9.
$$\begin{array}{r} 16 \\ +1 \\ \hline \end{array}$$

10.
$$\begin{array}{r} 16 \\ +16 \\ \hline \end{array}$$

11.
$$\begin{array}{r} 16 \\ +4 \\ \hline \end{array}$$

12.
$$\begin{array}{r} 16 \\ +12 \\ \hline \end{array}$$

13.
$$\begin{array}{r} 16 \\ +18 \\ \hline \end{array}$$

14.
$$\begin{array}{r} 16 \\ +3 \\ \hline \end{array}$$

15.
$$\begin{array}{r} 16 \\ +15 \\ \hline \end{array}$$

16.
$$\begin{array}{r} 16 \\ +7 \\ \hline \end{array}$$

17.
$$\begin{array}{r} 16 \\ +11 \\ \hline \end{array}$$

18.
$$\begin{array}{r} 16 \\ +9 \\ \hline \end{array}$$

19.
$$\begin{array}{r} 16 \\ +5 \\ \hline \end{array}$$

20.
$$\begin{array}{r} 16 \\ +20 \\ \hline \end{array}$$

IF87115 *Timed Math Tests*

Addition Challenge

Name _____ Date _____

Time _____ Score _____

🕐 My time goal is _____ .

1.
$$\begin{array}{r} \square \\ +\ 16 \\ \hline 32 \end{array}$$

2.
$$\begin{array}{r} \square \\ +\ 16 \\ \hline 24 \end{array}$$

3.
$$\begin{array}{r} \square \\ +\ 16 \\ \hline 20 \end{array}$$

4.
$$\begin{array}{r} \square \\ +\ 16 \\ \hline 16 \end{array}$$

5.
$$\begin{array}{r} \square \\ +\ 16 \\ \hline 21 \end{array}$$

6.
$$\begin{array}{r} \square \\ +\ 16 \\ \hline 33 \end{array}$$

7.
$$\begin{array}{r} \square \\ +\ 16 \\ \hline 26 \end{array}$$

8.
$$\begin{array}{r} \square \\ +\ 16 \\ \hline 22 \end{array}$$

9.
$$\begin{array}{r} \square \\ +\ 16 \\ \hline 28 \end{array}$$

10.
$$\begin{array}{r} \square \\ +\ 16 \\ \hline 18 \end{array}$$

11.
$$\begin{array}{r} \square \\ +\ 16 \\ \hline 30 \end{array}$$

12.
$$\begin{array}{r} \square \\ +\ 16 \\ \hline 23 \end{array}$$

13.
$$\begin{array}{r} \square \\ +\ 16 \\ \hline 35 \end{array}$$

14.
$$\begin{array}{r} \square \\ +\ 16 \\ \hline 29 \end{array}$$

15.
$$\begin{array}{r} \square \\ +\ 16 \\ \hline 27 \end{array}$$

16.
$$\begin{array}{r} \square \\ +\ 16 \\ \hline 19 \end{array}$$

17.
$$\begin{array}{r} \square \\ +\ 16 \\ \hline 25 \end{array}$$

18.
$$\begin{array}{r} \square \\ +\ 16 \\ \hline 17 \end{array}$$

19.
$$\begin{array}{r} \square \\ +\ 16 \\ \hline 31 \end{array}$$

20.
$$\begin{array}{r} \square \\ +\ 16 \\ \hline 34 \end{array}$$

IF87115 *Timed Math Tests*

Addition Pretest

Name _____ Date _____

Time _____ Score _____

My time goal is _____ .

1.
```
   20
+  17
```

2.
```
    5
+  17
```

3.
```
    9
+  17
```

4.
```
   11
+  17
```

5.
```
    7
+  17
```

6.
```
   15
+  17
```

7.
```
    3
+  17
```

8.
```
   18
+  17
```

9.
```
   12
+  17
```

10.
```
    4
+  17
```

11.
```
   16
+  17
```

12.
```
    1
+  17
```

13.
```
    8
+  17
```

14.
```
   14
+  17
```

15.
```
   19
+  17
```

16.
```
    6
+  17
```

17.
```
   10
+  17
```

18.
```
   13
+  17
```

19.
```
   17
+  17
```

20.
```
    2
+  17
```

IF87115 *Timed Math Tests*

Addition Practice

Name _____   Date _____

Time _____   Score _____

My time goal is _____ .

1.
$$17 + 2$$

2.
$$17 + 17$$

3.
$$17 + 13$$

4.
$$17 + 10$$

5.
$$17 + 6$$

6.
$$17 + 19$$

7.
$$17 + 14$$

8.
$$17 + 8$$

9.
$$17 + 1$$

10.
$$17 + 16$$

11.
$$17 + 4$$

12.
$$17 + 12$$

13.
$$17 + 18$$

14.
$$17 + 3$$

15.
$$17 + 15$$

16.
$$17 + 7$$

17.
$$17 + 11$$

18.
$$17 + 9$$

19.
$$17 + 5$$

20.
$$17 + 20$$

IF87115 *Timed Math Tests*

Addition Challenge

Name _____ Date _____

Time _____ Score _____

🕐 My time goal is _____ .

1. ☐
    + 17
    —
    21

2. ☐
    + 17
    —
    34

3. ☐
    + 17
    —
    31

4. ☐
    + 17
    —
    26

5. ☐
    + 17
    —
    33

6. ☐
    + 17
    —
    24

7. ☐
    + 17
    —
    35

8. ☐
    + 17
    —
    22

9. ☐
    + 17
    —
    28

10. ☐
    + 17
    —
    18

11. ☐
    + 17
    —
    20

12. ☐
    + 17
    —
    30

13. ☐
    + 17
    —
    23

14. ☐
    + 17
    —
    32

15. ☐
    + 17
    —
    29

16. ☐
    + 17
    —
    19

17. ☐
    + 17
    —
    27

18. ☐
    + 17
    —
    25

19. ☐
    + 17
    —
    31

20. ☐
    + 17
    —
    17

IF87115 *Timed Math Tests*

Addition Pretest

Name _____   Date _____

Time _____   Score _____

⏰ My time goal is _____ .

1. $\begin{array}{r} 2 \\ + 18 \\ \hline \end{array}$	2. $\begin{array}{r} 15 \\ + 18 \\ \hline \end{array}$	3. $\begin{array}{r} 9 \\ + 18 \\ \hline \end{array}$	4. $\begin{array}{r} 11 \\ + 18 \\ \hline \end{array}$	5. $\begin{array}{r} 17 \\ + 18 \\ \hline \end{array}$
6. $\begin{array}{r} 5 \\ + 18 \\ \hline \end{array}$	7. $\begin{array}{r} 13 \\ + 18 \\ \hline \end{array}$	8. $\begin{array}{r} 8 \\ + 18 \\ \hline \end{array}$	9. $\begin{array}{r} 12 \\ + 18 \\ \hline \end{array}$	10. $\begin{array}{r} 4 \\ + 18 \\ \hline \end{array}$
11. $\begin{array}{r} 6 \\ + 18 \\ \hline \end{array}$	12. $\begin{array}{r} 1 \\ + 18 \\ \hline \end{array}$	13. $\begin{array}{r} 18 \\ + 18 \\ \hline \end{array}$	14. $\begin{array}{r} 14 \\ + 18 \\ \hline \end{array}$	15. $\begin{array}{r} 19 \\ + 18 \\ \hline \end{array}$
16. $\begin{array}{r} 18 \\ + 18 \\ \hline \end{array}$	17. $\begin{array}{r} 14 \\ + 18 \\ \hline \end{array}$	18. $\begin{array}{r} 3 \\ + 18 \\ \hline \end{array}$	19. $\begin{array}{r} 7 \\ + 18 \\ \hline \end{array}$	20. $\begin{array}{r} 20 \\ + 18 \\ \hline \end{array}$

IF87115 *Timed Math Tests*

Addition Practice

Name _____   Date _____

Time _____   Score _____

My time goal is _____ .

1.
$$18 + 2$$

2.
$$18 + 7$$

3.
$$18 + 13$$

4.
$$18 + 10$$

5.
$$18 + 6$$

6.
$$18 + 19$$

7.
$$18 + 14$$

8.
$$18 + 8$$

9.
$$18 + 1$$

10.
$$18 + 16$$

11.
$$18 + 4$$

12.
$$18 + 12$$

13.
$$18 + 18$$

14.
$$18 + 3$$

15.
$$18 + 15$$

16.
$$18 + 7$$

17.
$$18 + 11$$

18.
$$18 + 9$$

19.
$$18 + 5$$

20.
$$18 + 20$$

Addition Challenge

Name _____ Date _____

Time _____ Score _____

⏰ My time goal is _____ .

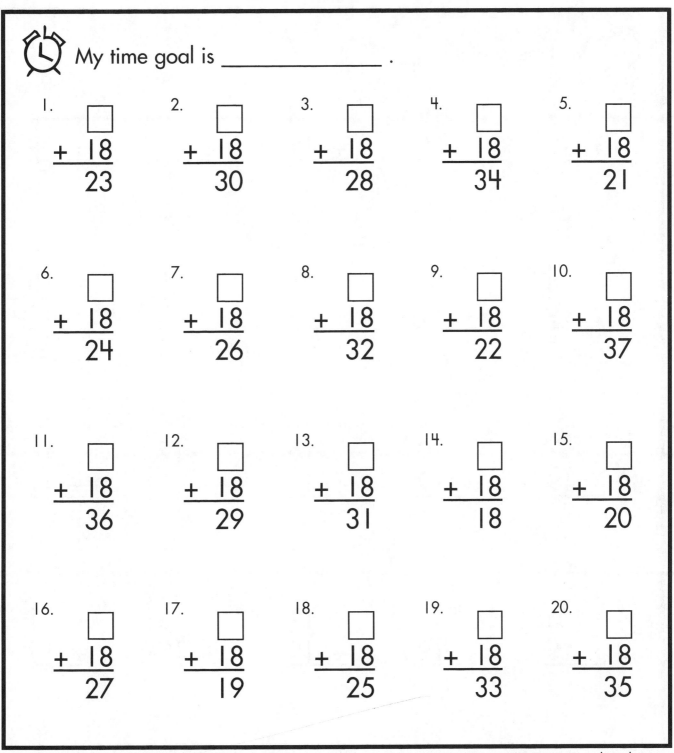

1. ☐
    + 18
    ──
    23

2. ☐
    + 18
    ──
    30

3. ☐
    + 18
    ──
    28

4. ☐
    + 18
    ──
    34

5. ☐
    + 18
    ──
    21

6. ☐
    + 18
    ──
    24

7. ☐
    + 18
    ──
    26

8. ☐
    + 18
    ──
    32

9. ☐
    + 18
    ──
    22

10. ☐
    + 18
    ──
    37

11. ☐
    + 18
    ──
    36

12. ☐
    + 18
    ──
    29

13. ☐
    + 18
    ──
    31

14. ☐
    + 18
    ──
    18

15. ☐
    + 18
    ──
    20

16. ☐
    + 18
    ──
    27

17. ☐
    + 18
    ──
    19

18. ☐
    + 18
    ──
    25

19. ☐
    + 18
    ──
    33

20. ☐
    + 18
    ──
    35

IF87115 *Timed Math Tests*

Addition Pretest

Name _____ Date _____

Time _____ Score _____

🕐 My time goal is _____ .

1. 9 + 19	2. 19 + 19	3. 4 + 19	4. 6 + 19	5. 2 + 19
6. 8 + 19	7. 10 + 19	8. 16 + 19	9. 5 + 19	10. 14 + 19
11. 7 + 19	12. 20 + 19	13. 15 + 19	14. 12 + 19	15. 18 + 19
16. 3 + 19	17. 17 + 19	18. 11 + 19	19. 13 + 19	20. 1 + 19

IF87115 *Timed Math Tests*

Addition Practice

Name _____   Date _____

Time _____   Score _____

🕐 My time goal is _____ .

1. 19 + 7	2. 19 + 17	3. 19 + 20	4. 19 + 15	5. 19 + 12
6. 19 + 18	7. 19 + 3	8. 19 + 1	9. 19 + 11	10. 19 + 13
11. 19 + 4	12. 19 + 5	13. 19 + 16	14. 19 + 10	15. 19 + 8
16. 19 + 2	17. 19 + 6	18. 19 + 4	19. 19 + 19	20. 19 + 9

IF87115 *Timed Math Tests*

Addition Challenge

Name _____   Date _____

Time _____   Score _____

🕐 My time goal is _____ .

1.
$$\begin{array}{r} \square \\ +\ 19 \\ \hline 21 \end{array}$$

2.
$$\begin{array}{r} \square \\ +\ 19 \\ \hline 32 \end{array}$$

3.
$$\begin{array}{r} \square \\ +\ 19 \\ \hline 25 \end{array}$$

4.
$$\begin{array}{r} \square \\ +\ 19 \\ \hline 34 \end{array}$$

5.
$$\begin{array}{r} \square \\ +\ 19 \\ \hline 24 \end{array}$$

6.
$$\begin{array}{r} \square \\ +\ 19 \\ \hline 35 \end{array}$$

7.
$$\begin{array}{r} \square \\ +\ 19 \\ \hline 22 \end{array}$$

8.
$$\begin{array}{r} \square \\ +\ 19 \\ \hline 28 \end{array}$$

9.
$$\begin{array}{r} \square \\ +\ 19 \\ \hline 37 \end{array}$$

10.
$$\begin{array}{r} \square \\ +\ 19 \\ \hline 26 \end{array}$$

11.
$$\begin{array}{r} \square \\ +\ 19 \\ \hline 20 \end{array}$$

12.
$$\begin{array}{r} \square \\ +\ 19 \\ \hline 30 \end{array}$$

13.
$$\begin{array}{r} \square \\ +\ 19 \\ \hline 23 \end{array}$$

14.
$$\begin{array}{r} \square \\ +\ 19 \\ \hline 36 \end{array}$$

15.
$$\begin{array}{r} \square \\ +\ 19 \\ \hline 31 \end{array}$$

16.
$$\begin{array}{r} \square \\ +\ 19 \\ \hline 27 \end{array}$$

17.
$$\begin{array}{r} \square \\ +\ 19 \\ \hline 19 \end{array}$$

18.
$$\begin{array}{r} \square \\ +\ 19 \\ \hline 29 \end{array}$$

19.
$$\begin{array}{r} \square \\ +\ 19 \\ \hline 33 \end{array}$$

20.
$$\begin{array}{r} \square \\ +\ 19 \\ \hline 38 \end{array}$$

IF87115 *Timed Math Tests*

Addition Review

Name _____   Date _____

Time _____   Score _____

My time goal is _____ .

1.
$$\begin{array}{r} 4 \\ +\ 4 \\ \hline \end{array}$$

2.
$$\begin{array}{r} 8 \\ +\ 5 \\ \hline \end{array}$$

3.
$$\begin{array}{r} 2 \\ +\ 3 \\ \hline \end{array}$$

4.
$$\begin{array}{r} 20 \\ +\ 6 \\ \hline \end{array}$$

5.
$$\begin{array}{r} 11 \\ +\ 3 \\ \hline \end{array}$$

6.
$$\begin{array}{r} 7 \\ +\ 6 \\ \hline \end{array}$$

7.
$$\begin{array}{r} 16 \\ +\ 4 \\ \hline \end{array}$$

8.
$$\begin{array}{r} 3 \\ +\ 4 \\ \hline \end{array}$$

9.
$$\begin{array}{r} 18 \\ +\ 5 \\ \hline \end{array}$$

10.
$$\begin{array}{r} 10 \\ +\ 2 \\ \hline \end{array}$$

11.
$$\begin{array}{r} 19 \\ +\ 3 \\ \hline \end{array}$$

12.
$$\begin{array}{r} 13 \\ +\ 3 \\ \hline \end{array}$$

13.
$$\begin{array}{r} 14 \\ +\ 4 \\ \hline \end{array}$$

14.
$$\begin{array}{r} 19 \\ +\ 6 \\ \hline \end{array}$$

15.
$$\begin{array}{r} 5 \\ +\ 3 \\ \hline \end{array}$$

16.
$$\begin{array}{r} 5 \\ +\ 5 \\ \hline \end{array}$$

17.
$$\begin{array}{r} 13 \\ +\ 2 \\ \hline \end{array}$$

18.
$$\begin{array}{r} 9 \\ +\ 6 \\ \hline \end{array}$$

19.
$$\begin{array}{r} 12 \\ +\ 3 \\ \hline \end{array}$$

20.
$$\begin{array}{r} 15 \\ +\ 3 \\ \hline \end{array}$$

Addition Review

Name _____   Date _____

Time _____   Score _____

My time goal is _____ .

1.	2.	3.	4.	5.
3 + 10	9 + 7	9 + 8	15 + 9	7 + 7

6.	7.	8.	9.	10.
11 + 10	5 + 7	6 + 9	6 + 7	18 + 8

11.	12.	13.	14.	15.
5 + 7	13 + 9	15 + 10	11 + 7	3 + 11

16.	17.	18.	19.	20.
5 + 9	12 + 8	14 + 7	9 + 11	13 + 8

IF87115 *Timed Math Tests*

Mixed +12, +13, +14, +15, and +16

Addition Review

Name _____   Date _____

Time _____   Score _____

My time goal is _____ .

1. $\begin{array}{r} 5 \\ + 15 \\ \hline \end{array}$
2. $\begin{array}{r} 15 \\ + 14 \\ \hline \end{array}$
3. $\begin{array}{r} 2 \\ + 15 \\ \hline \end{array}$
4. $\begin{array}{r} 14 \\ + 16 \\ \hline \end{array}$
5. $\begin{array}{r} 11 \\ + 12 \\ \hline \end{array}$

6. $\begin{array}{r} 18 \\ + 15 \\ \hline \end{array}$
7. $\begin{array}{r} 3 \\ + 13 \\ \hline \end{array}$
8. $\begin{array}{r} 3 \\ + 12 \\ \hline \end{array}$
9. $\begin{array}{r} 18 \\ + 14 \\ \hline \end{array}$
10. $\begin{array}{r} 10 \\ + 15 \\ \hline \end{array}$

11. $\begin{array}{r} 7 \\ + 13 \\ \hline \end{array}$
12. $\begin{array}{r} 12 \\ + 14 \\ \hline \end{array}$
13. $\begin{array}{r} 8 \\ + 12 \\ \hline \end{array}$
14. $\begin{array}{r} 11 \\ + 14 \\ \hline \end{array}$
15. $\begin{array}{r} 4 \\ + 17 \\ \hline \end{array}$

16. $\begin{array}{r} 20 \\ + 15 \\ \hline \end{array}$
17. $\begin{array}{r} 9 \\ + 14 \\ \hline \end{array}$
18. $\begin{array}{r} 9 \\ + 13 \\ \hline \end{array}$
19. $\begin{array}{r} 19 \\ + 14 \\ \hline \end{array}$
20. $\begin{array}{r} 12 \\ + 15 \\ \hline \end{array}$

IF87115 *Timed Math Tests*

Addition Review

Name _____ Date _____

Time _____ Score _____

My time goal is _____ .

1.
$$16$$
$$+\ 17$$

2.
$$2$$
$$+\ 18$$

3.
$$16$$
$$+\ 16$$

4.
$$9$$
$$+\ 17$$

5.
$$15$$
$$+\ 17$$

6.
$$7$$
$$+\ 18$$

7.
$$5$$
$$+\ 17$$

8.
$$19$$
$$+\ 20$$

9.
$$8$$
$$+\ 16$$

10.
$$3$$
$$+\ 19$$

11.
$$19$$
$$+\ 17$$

12.
$$17$$
$$+\ 20$$

13.
$$4$$
$$+\ 18$$

14.
$$13$$
$$+\ 17$$

15.
$$3$$
$$+\ 16$$

16.
$$19$$
$$+\ 18$$

17.
$$10$$
$$+\ 19$$

18.
$$5$$
$$+\ 16$$

19.
$$4$$
$$+\ 17$$

20.
$$7$$
$$+\ 17$$

Answer Key

+2A ══════
11, 4, 22, 20, 13,
12, 17, 6, 16, 21,
7, 15, 9, 3, 5,
19, 8, 14, 18, 10

+2B ══════
10, 18, 14, 8, 19,
5, 3, 9, 15, 7,
21, 16, 6, 17, 12,
13, 20, 22, 4, 11

+2C ══════
19, 12, 8, 4, 10,
2, 14, 0, 6, 16,
18, 9, 1, 13, 7,
5, 17, 3, 11, 15

+3A ══════
20, 22, 7, 9, 5,
11, 13, 19, 8, 17,
10, 23, 18, 15, 21,
12, 6, 4, 14, 16

+3B ══════
10, 20, 23, 18, 15,
21, 6, 4, 14, 16,
17, 8, 19, 13, 11,
5, 9, 7, 22, 12

+3C ══════
6, 16, 9, 0, 2,
4, 8, 1, 17, 3,
15, 12, 8, 10, 7,
13, 11, 14, 5, 4

+4A ══════
24, 9, 13, 15, 11,
19, 7, 22, 16, 8,
20, 5, 12, 18, 23,
10, 14, 17, 21, 6

+4B ══════
6, 21, 17, 14, 10,
23, 18, 12, 5, 20,
8, 16, 22, 7, 19,
11, 15, 13, 9, 24

+4C ══════
17, 10, 6, 2, 8,
20, 12, 18, 4, 14,
16, 7, 19, 11, 5,
3, 15, 1, 9, 13

+5A ══════
7, 20, 14, 16, 22,
10, 18, 13, 20, 9,
11, 6, 23, 19, 24,
21, 15, 8, 12, 25

+5B ══════
7, 22, 18, 15, 11,
24, 19, 13, 6, 21,
9, 17, 23, 8, 20,
12, 16, 14, 10, 25

+5C ══════
6, 9, 15, 11, 16,
19, 1, 17, 3, 13,
5, 7, 18, 10, 4,
2, 14, 20, 8, 12

+6A ══════
26, 11, 15, 17, 13,
21, 9, 24, 18, 10,
22, 7, 14, 20, 25,
12, 16, 19, 23, 8

+6B ══════
8, 23, 19, 16, 12,
25, 20, 14, 7, 22,
10, 18, 24, 9, 21,
13, 17, 15, 11, 26

+6C ══════
15, 8, 4, 0, 6,
18, 10, 16 , 2, 12,
14, 5, 17, 9, 3,
1, 13, 19, 7, 11

+7A ══════
9, 22, 16, 18, 24,
12, 20, 15, 19, 11,
13, 8, 25, 24, 26,
23, 17, 10, 14, 27

+7B ══════
9, 24, 20, 17, 13,
26, 21, 15, 8, 23,
11, 19, 25, 10, 22,
14, 18, 16, 12, 27

+7C ══════
4, 7, 13, 9, 14,
17, 19, 15, 1, 11,
3, 5, 16, 8, 2,
20, 12, 18, 6, 10

+8A ══════
28, 13, 17, 19, 15,
23, 11, 26, 20, 12,
24, 9, 16, 22, 27,
14, 18, 21, 25, 10

+8B ══════
10, 25, 21, 18, 14,
27, 22, 16, 9, 24,
12, 20, 26, 11, 23,
15, 19, 17, 13, 28

+8C ══════
13, 6, 2, 18, 4,
16, 8, 14, 0, 10,
12, 3, 15, 7, 1,
19, 11, 17, 5, 9

+9A ══════
11, 24, 18, 20, 26,
14, 22, 17, 21, 13,
15, 10, 27, 23, 28,
25, 19, 12, 16, 29

+9B ══════
11, 26, 22, 19, 15,
28, 23, 17, 10, 25,
13, 21, 27, 12, 24,
16, 20, 18, 14, 29

+9C ══════
2, 5, 11, 7, 12,
15, 17, 13, 16, 9,
1, 3, 14, 6, 0,
18, 10, 16, 4, 8

+10A ══════
19, 29, 14, 16, 12,
18, 20, 26, 15, 24,
17, 30, 25, 22, 28,
13, 27, 21, 23, 11

+10B ══════
17, 27, 30, 25, 22,
28, 13, 11, 21, 23,
24, 15, 26, 20, 18,
12, 16, 14, 29, 19

+10C ══════
11, 9, 2, 13, 5,
15, 1, 12, 10, 16,
8, 14, 19, 3, 0,
6, 17, 7, 18, 4,

+11A ══════
31, 16, 20, 22, 18,
26, 14, 29, 23, 15,
27, 12, 19, 25, 30,
17, 21, 24, 28, 13

+11B ══════
13, 28, 27, 21, 17,
30, 25, 19, 12, 27,
15, 23, 29, 14, 26,
18, 22, 20, 16, 31

+11C ══════
10, 3, 1, 14, 13,
5, 11, 17, 7, 15,
9, 0, 12, 4, 19,
16, 8, 18, 2, 6

+12A ══════
18, 13, 30, 26, 31,
28, 22, 15, 19, 32,
16, 24, 20, 25, 17,
29, 23, 21, 27, 14

+12B ══════
14, 29, 25, 22, 23,
18, 31, 26, 20, 13,
28, 16, 24, 30, 15,
27, 19, 21, 17, 32

+12C ══════
0, 2, 8, 4, 9,
12, 4, 10, 16, 6,
18, 11, 3, 17, 15,
7, 13, 1, 5, 19

+13A ══════
33, 18, 22, 24, 20,
28, 16, 31, 25, 17,
29, 14, 21, 27, 32,
19, 23, 26, 30, 15

+13B ══════
15, 30, 26, 23, 19,
32, 27, 21, 14, 29,
17, 25, 31, 16, 28,
20, 24, 22, 18, 33

© Frank Schaffer Publications

IF87115 *Timed Math Tests*

Answer Key

+13C ===========
8, 1, 18, 13, 0,
11, 3, 9, 15, 5,
7, 17, 10, 2, 16,
6, 14, 12, 0, 4

+14A ===========
16, 29, 23, 25, 31,
19, 27, 22, 26, 18,
20, 15, 32, 28, 33,
30, 24, 17, 21, 34

+14B ===========
16, 31, 27, 24, 20,
33, 28, 22, 15, 20,
18, 26, 32, 17, 29,
21, 25, 23, 19, 34

+14C ===========
9, 16, 14, 2, 7,
10, 12, 18, 8, 4,
0, 15, 17, 1, 6,
13, 5, 11, 19, 3

+15A ===========
24, 34, 19, 21, 17,
23, 25, 31, 20, 29,
22, 35, 30, 27, 33,
18, 32, 26, 28, 16

+15B ===========
22, 32, 35, 30, 27,
33, 18, 16, 26, 28,
29, 20, 31, 25, 23,
17, 21, 19, 34, 24

+15C ===========
6, 17, 10, 19, 9,
1, 7, 13, 3, 11,
5, 15, 8, 0, 16,
12, 4, 14, 18, 2

+16A ===========
22, 17, 34, 30, 35,
32, 26, 19, 23, 36,
20, 28, 24, 29, 21,
33, 27, 25, 31, 18

+16B ===========
18, 33, 29, 26, 22,
35, 30, 24, 17, 32,
20, 28, 34, 19, 31,
23, 27, 25, 21, 36

+16C ===========
16, 8, 4, 0, 5,
17, 10, 6, 12, 2,
14, 7, 19, 13, 11,
3, 9, 1, 15, 18

+17A ===========
37, 22, 26, 28, 24,
32, 20, 35, 29, 21,
33, 18, 25, 31, 36,
23, 27, 30, 34, 19

+17B ===========
19, 34, 30, 27, 23,
36, 31, 25, 18, 33,
21, 29, 35, 20, 32,
24, 28, 26, 22, 37

+17C ===========
4, 17, 14, 9, 16,
7, 18, 5, 11, 1,
3, 13, 6, 15, 12,
2, 10, 8, 14, 0

+18A ===========
20, 33, 27, 29, 35,
23, 31, 26, 30, 22,
24, 19, 36, 32, 37,
36, 32, 21, 25, 38

+18B ===========
20, 25, 31, 28, 24,
37, 32, 26, 19, 34,
22, 30, 36, 21, 33,
25, 29, 27, 23, 38

+ 18C ===========
5, 12, 10, 16, 3,
6, 8, 14, 4, 19,
18, 11, 13, 0, 2,
9, 1, 7, 15, 17

+19A ===========
28, 38, 23, 25, 21,
27, 29, 35, 24, 33,
26, 39, 34, 31, 37,
22, 36 30, 32, 20

+19B ===========
26, 36, 39, 34, 31,
37, 22, 20, 30, 32,
23, 24, 35, 29, 27,
21, 25, 23, 38, 28

+19C ===========
2, 13, 6, 15, 5,
16, 3, 9, 18, 7,
1, 11, 4, 17, 12,
8, 0, 10, 14, 19

Review A ========
8, 13, 5, 26, 14,
13, 20, 7, 23, 12,
22, 16, 18, 25, 8,
10, 15, 15, 15, 18

Review B ========
13, 16, 17, 24, 14,
21, 12, 15, 13, 26,
12, 22, 25, 18, 14
14, 20, 21, 20, 21

Review C ========
20, 29, 17, 30, 23,
33, 16, 15, 32, 25,
20, 26, 20, 25, 21,
35, 23, 22, 33, 27

Review D ========
33, 20, 32, 26, 32,
25, 22, 39, 24, 22,
36, 37, 22, 30, 19,
37, 29, 21, 21, 24

IF87115 *Timed Math Tests*

Name_____

Subtraction Record Chart

Test	Time	Score	Time	Score
−2A				
−2B				
−2C				
−3A				
−3B				
−3C				
−4A				
−4B				
−4C				
−5A				
−5B				
−5C				
−6A				
−6B				
−6C				
−7A				
−7B				
−7C				
−8A				
−8B				
−8C				
−9A				
−9B				
−9C				
−10A				
−10B				
−10C				
−11A				
−11B				
−11C				
−12A				
−12B				
−12C				

IF87115 *Timed Math Tests*

Subtraction Record Chart (cont.)

Test	Time	Score	Time	Score
−13A				
−13B				
−13C				
−14A				
−14B				
−14C				
−15A				
−15B				
−15C				
−16A				
−16B				
−16C				
−17A				
−17B				
−17C				
−18A				
−18B				
−18C				
−19A				
−19B				
−19C				
Review A				
Review B				
Review C				
Review D				

IF87115 *Timed Math Tests*

Subtraction Pretest

Name _____   Date _____

Time _____   Score _____

⏰ My time goal is _____ .

1. 3
  − 2

2. 7
  − 2

3. 10
  − 2

4. 4
  − 2

5. 5
  − 2

6. 18
  − 2

7. 8
  − 2

8. 20
  − 2

9. 16
  − 2

10. 2
  − 2

11. 12
  − 2

12. 6
  − 2

13. 11
  − 2

14. 9
  − 2

15. 13
  − 2

16. 19
  − 2

17. 15
  − 2

18. 12
  − 2

19. 17
  − 2

20. 14
  − 2

IF87115 *Timed Math Tests*

Subtraction/Addition Practice −2B

Name _____ Date _____

Time _____ Score _____

My time goal is _____ .

1. $\begin{array}{r} 19 \\ + 2 \\ \hline \end{array}$
2. $\begin{array}{r} 2 \\ - 2 \\ \hline \end{array}$
3. $\begin{array}{r} 10 \\ - 2 \\ \hline \end{array}$
4. $\begin{array}{r} 15 \\ + 2 \\ \hline \end{array}$
5. $\begin{array}{r} 8 \\ - 2 \\ \hline \end{array}$

6. $\begin{array}{r} 5 \\ + 2 \\ \hline \end{array}$
7. $\begin{array}{r} 7 \\ + 2 \\ \hline \end{array}$
8. $\begin{array}{r} 18 \\ - 2 \\ \hline \end{array}$
9. $\begin{array}{r} 9 \\ - 2 \\ \hline \end{array}$
10. $\begin{array}{r} 14 \\ - 2 \\ \hline \end{array}$

11. $\begin{array}{r} 16 \\ + 2 \\ \hline \end{array}$
12. $\begin{array}{r} 4 \\ + 2 \\ \hline \end{array}$
13. $\begin{array}{r} 11 \\ - 2 \\ \hline \end{array}$
14. $\begin{array}{r} 15 \\ - 2 \\ \hline \end{array}$
15. $\begin{array}{r} 17 \\ - 2 \\ \hline \end{array}$

16. $\begin{array}{r} 13 \\ + 2 \\ \hline \end{array}$
17. $\begin{array}{r} 20 \\ - 2 \\ \hline \end{array}$
18. $\begin{array}{r} 12 \\ - 2 \\ \hline \end{array}$
19. $\begin{array}{r} 14 \\ + 2 \\ \hline \end{array}$
20. $\begin{array}{r} 6 \\ - 2 \\ \hline \end{array}$

IF87115 *Timed Math Tests*

Subtraction Challenge

Name _____   Date _____

Time _____   Score _____

⏰ My time goal is _____ .

1.
$$\begin{array}{r} \square \\ -\ 2 \\ \hline 12 \end{array}$$

2.
$$\begin{array}{r} \square \\ -\ 2 \\ \hline 15 \end{array}$$

3.
$$\begin{array}{r} \square \\ -\ 2 \\ \hline 10 \end{array}$$

4.
$$\begin{array}{r} \square \\ -\ 2 \\ \hline 13 \end{array}$$

5.
$$\begin{array}{r} \square \\ -\ 2 \\ \hline 17 \end{array}$$

6.
$$\begin{array}{r} \square \\ -\ 2 \\ \hline 11 \end{array}$$

7.
$$\begin{array}{r} \square \\ -\ 2 \\ \hline 12 \end{array}$$

8.
$$\begin{array}{r} \square \\ -\ 2 \\ \hline 10 \end{array}$$

9.
$$\begin{array}{r} \square \\ -\ 2 \\ \hline 0 \end{array}$$

10.
$$\begin{array}{r} \square \\ -\ 2 \\ \hline 4 \end{array}$$

11.
$$\begin{array}{r} \square \\ -\ 2 \\ \hline 18 \end{array}$$

12.
$$\begin{array}{r} \square \\ -\ 2 \\ \hline 6 \end{array}$$

13.
$$\begin{array}{r} \square \\ -\ 2 \\ \hline 16 \end{array}$$

14.
$$\begin{array}{r} \square \\ -\ 2 \\ \hline 3 \end{array}$$

15.
$$\begin{array}{r} \square \\ -\ 2 \\ \hline 2 \end{array}$$

16.
$$\begin{array}{r} \square \\ -\ 2 \\ \hline 7 \end{array}$$

17.
$$\begin{array}{r} \square \\ -\ 2 \\ \hline 8 \end{array}$$

18.
$$\begin{array}{r} \square \\ -\ 2 \\ \hline 5 \end{array}$$

19.
$$\begin{array}{r} \square \\ -\ 2 \\ \hline 1 \end{array}$$

20.
$$\begin{array}{r} \square \\ -\ 2 \\ \hline 9 \end{array}$$

IF87115 *Timed Math Tests*

Subtraction Pretest

Name _____   Date _____

Time _____   Score _____

My time goal is _____ .

1. $\begin{array}{r} 15 \\ -\ 3 \\ \hline \end{array}$	2. $\begin{array}{r} 12 \\ -\ 3 \\ \hline \end{array}$	3. $\begin{array}{r} 6 \\ -\ 3 \\ \hline \end{array}$	4. $\begin{array}{r} 4 \\ -\ 3 \\ \hline \end{array}$	5. $\begin{array}{r} 9 \\ -\ 3 \\ \hline \end{array}$
6. $\begin{array}{r} 17 \\ -\ 3 \\ \hline \end{array}$	7. $\begin{array}{r} 3 \\ -\ 3 \\ \hline \end{array}$	8. $\begin{array}{r} 20 \\ -\ 3 \\ \hline \end{array}$	9. $\begin{array}{r} 14 \\ -\ 3 \\ \hline \end{array}$	10. $\begin{array}{r} 18 \\ -\ 3 \\ \hline \end{array}$
11. $\begin{array}{r} 5 \\ -\ 3 \\ \hline \end{array}$	12. $\begin{array}{r} 16 \\ -\ 3 \\ \hline \end{array}$	13. $\begin{array}{r} 7 \\ -\ 3 \\ \hline \end{array}$	14. $\begin{array}{r} 11 \\ -\ 3 \\ \hline \end{array}$	15. $\begin{array}{r} 8 \\ -\ 3 \\ \hline \end{array}$
16. $\begin{array}{r} 6 \\ -\ 3 \\ \hline \end{array}$	17. $\begin{array}{r} 10 \\ -\ 3 \\ \hline \end{array}$	18. $\begin{array}{r} 13 \\ -\ 3 \\ \hline \end{array}$	19. $\begin{array}{r} 19 \\ -\ 3 \\ \hline \end{array}$	20. $\begin{array}{r} 12 \\ -\ 3 \\ \hline \end{array}$

Subtraction/Addition Practice   –3B

Name _____   Date _____

Time _____   Score _____

My time goal is _____ .

1. $\begin{array}{r} 19 \\ -\ 3 \\ \hline \end{array}$
2. $\begin{array}{r} 3 \\ -\ 3 \\ \hline \end{array}$
3. $\begin{array}{r} 16 \\ +\ 3 \\ \hline \end{array}$
4. $\begin{array}{r} 13 \\ -\ 3 \\ \hline \end{array}$
5. $\begin{array}{r} 8 \\ -\ 3 \\ \hline \end{array}$

6. $\begin{array}{r} 14 \\ +\ 3 \\ \hline \end{array}$
7. $\begin{array}{r} 17 \\ -\ 3 \\ \hline \end{array}$
8. $\begin{array}{r} 12 \\ -\ 3 \\ \hline \end{array}$
9. $\begin{array}{r} 4 \\ +\ 3 \\ \hline \end{array}$
10. $\begin{array}{r} 19 \\ +\ 3 \\ \hline \end{array}$

11. $\begin{array}{r} 15 \\ -\ 3 \\ \hline \end{array}$
12. $\begin{array}{r} 11 \\ +\ 3 \\ \hline \end{array}$
13. $\begin{array}{r} 18 \\ -\ 3 \\ \hline \end{array}$
14. $\begin{array}{r} 13 \\ +\ 3 \\ \hline \end{array}$
15. $\begin{array}{r} 6 \\ +\ 3 \\ \hline \end{array}$

16. $\begin{array}{r} 10 \\ -\ 3 \\ \hline \end{array}$
17. $\begin{array}{r} 9 \\ -\ 3 \\ \hline \end{array}$
18. $\begin{array}{r} 7 \\ +\ 3 \\ \hline \end{array}$
19. $\begin{array}{r} 20 \\ -\ 3 \\ \hline \end{array}$
20. $\begin{array}{r} 5 \\ -\ 3 \\ \hline \end{array}$

IF87115 *Timed Math Tests*

Subtraction Challenge

Name _____   Date _____

Time _____   Score _____

🕐 My time goal is _____ .

1.
$$\boxed{} \\ -\,3 \\ \hline 9$$

2.
$$\boxed{} \\ -\,3 \\ \hline 19$$

3.
$$\boxed{} \\ -\,3 \\ \hline 5$$

4.
$$\boxed{} \\ -\,3 \\ \hline 8$$

5.
$$\boxed{} \\ -\,3 \\ \hline 7$$

6.
$$\boxed{} \\ -\,3 \\ \hline 2$$

7.
$$\boxed{} \\ -\,3 \\ \hline 16$$

8.
$$\boxed{} \\ -\,3 \\ \hline 6$$

9.
$$\boxed{} \\ -\,3 \\ \hline 3$$

10.
$$\boxed{} \\ -\,3 \\ \hline 18$$

11.
$$\boxed{} \\ -\,3 \\ \hline 14$$

12.
$$\boxed{} \\ -\,3 \\ \hline 1$$

13.
$$\boxed{} \\ -\,3 \\ \hline 10$$

14.
$$\boxed{} \\ -\,3 \\ \hline 4$$

15.
$$\boxed{} \\ -\,3 \\ \hline 11$$

16.
$$\boxed{} \\ -\,3 \\ \hline 17$$

17.
$$\boxed{} \\ -\,3 \\ \hline 13$$

18.
$$\boxed{} \\ -\,3 \\ \hline 20$$

19.
$$\boxed{} \\ -\,3 \\ \hline 15$$

20.
$$\boxed{} \\ -\,3 \\ \hline 12$$

IF87115 *Timed Math Tests*

Subtraction Pretest

Name _____   Date _____

Time _____   Score _____

🕐 My time goal is _____ .

1.
$$8 - 4$$

2.
$$19 - 4$$

3.
$$13 - 4$$

4.
$$10 - 4$$

5.
$$6 - 4$$

6.
$$11 - 4$$

7.
$$21 - 4$$

8.
$$7 - 4$$

9.
$$16 - 4$$

10.
$$5 - 4$$

11.
$$15 - 4$$

12.
$$22 - 4$$

13.
$$9 - 4$$

14.
$$17 - 4$$

15.
$$20 - 4$$

16.
$$14 - 4$$

17.
$$18 - 4$$

18.
$$11 - 4$$

19.
$$12 - 4$$

20.
$$23 - 4$$

IF87115 *Timed Math Tests*

Subtraction/Addition Practice

Name _____   Date _____

Time _____   Score _____

🕐 My time goal is _____ .

1. 8 + 4	2. 11 + 4	3. 18 − 4	4. 5 + 4	5. 20 − 4
6. 19 + 4	7. 8 − 4	8. 9 + 4	9. 17 − 4	10. 10 − 4
11. 18 − 4	12. 16 − 4	13. 13 − 4	14. 20 + 4	15. 4 + 4
16. 19 − 4	17. 14 − 4	18. 6 + 4	19. 13 + 4	20. 11 − 4

IF87115 *Timed Math Tests*

Subtraction Challenge

Name _____ Date _____

Time _____ Score _____

🕐 My time goal is _____ .

1.
$$\begin{array}{r}\Box \\ -\ 4 \\ \hline 15 \end{array}$$

2.
$$\begin{array}{r}\Box \\ -\ 4 \\ \hline 12 \end{array}$$

3.
$$\begin{array}{r}\Box \\ -\ 4 \\ \hline 20 \end{array}$$

4.
$$\begin{array}{r}\Box \\ -\ 4 \\ \hline 13 \end{array}$$

5.
$$\begin{array}{r}\Box \\ -\ 4 \\ \hline 17 \end{array}$$

6.
$$\begin{array}{r}\Box \\ -\ 4 \\ \hline 11 \end{array}$$

7.
$$\begin{array}{r}\Box \\ -\ 4 \\ \hline 10 \end{array}$$

8.
$$\begin{array}{r}\Box \\ -\ 4 \\ \hline 4 \end{array}$$

9.
$$\begin{array}{r}\Box \\ -\ 4 \\ \hline 1 \end{array}$$

10.
$$\begin{array}{r}\Box \\ -\ 4 \\ \hline 14 \end{array}$$

11.
$$\begin{array}{r}\Box \\ -\ 4 \\ \hline 18 \end{array}$$

12.
$$\begin{array}{r}\Box \\ -\ 4 \\ \hline 3 \end{array}$$

13.
$$\begin{array}{r}\Box \\ -\ 4 \\ \hline 6 \end{array}$$

14.
$$\begin{array}{r}\Box \\ -\ 4 \\ \hline 16 \end{array}$$

15.
$$\begin{array}{r}\Box \\ -\ 4 \\ \hline 2 \end{array}$$

16.
$$\begin{array}{r}\Box \\ -\ 4 \\ \hline 7 \end{array}$$

17.
$$\begin{array}{r}\Box \\ -\ 4 \\ \hline 8 \end{array}$$

18.
$$\begin{array}{r}\Box \\ -\ 4 \\ \hline 5 \end{array}$$

19.
$$\begin{array}{r}\Box \\ -\ 4 \\ \hline 19 \end{array}$$

20.
$$\begin{array}{r}\Box \\ -\ 4 \\ \hline 9 \end{array}$$

IF87115 *Timed Math Tests*

Subtraction Pretest

Name _____ Date _____

Time _____ Score _____

🕐 My time goal is _____ .

1.   15
   − 5

2.   12
   − 5

3.   6
   − 5

4.   9
   − 5

5.   17
   − 5

6.   20
   − 5

7.   14
   − 5

8.   18
   − 5

9.   5
   − 5

10.   8
   − 5

11.   16
   − 5

12.   7
   − 5

13.   11
   − 5

14.   8
   − 5

15.   6
   − 5

16.   10
   − 5

17.   13
   − 5

18.   19
   − 5

19.   12
   − 5

20.   18
   − 5

IF87115 *Timed Math Tests*

Mixed −5 and +5

Subtraction/Addition Practice −5B

Name _____ Date _____

Time _____ Score _____

🕐 My time goal is _____ .

1. $\begin{array}{r} 3 \\ +\ 5 \\ \hline \end{array}$
2. $\begin{array}{r} 17 \\ -\ 5 \\ \hline \end{array}$
3. $\begin{array}{r} 10 \\ -\ 5 \\ \hline \end{array}$
4. $\begin{array}{r} 14 \\ +\ 5 \\ \hline \end{array}$
5. $\begin{array}{r} 5 \\ +\ 5 \\ \hline \end{array}$

6. $\begin{array}{r} 13 \\ -\ 5 \\ \hline \end{array}$
7. $\begin{array}{r} 20 \\ +\ 5 \\ \hline \end{array}$
8. $\begin{array}{r} 7 \\ -\ 5 \\ \hline \end{array}$
9. $\begin{array}{r} 11 \\ +\ 5 \\ \hline \end{array}$
10. $\begin{array}{r} 8 \\ -\ 5 \\ \hline \end{array}$

11. $\begin{array}{r} 18 \\ -\ 5 \\ \hline \end{array}$
12. $\begin{array}{r} 11 \\ -\ 5 \\ \hline \end{array}$
13. $\begin{array}{r} 2 \\ +\ 5 \\ \hline \end{array}$
14. $\begin{array}{r} 19 \\ +\ 5 \\ \hline \end{array}$
15. $\begin{array}{r} 12 \\ -\ 5 \\ \hline \end{array}$

16. $\begin{array}{r} 15 \\ -\ 5 \\ \hline \end{array}$
17. $\begin{array}{r} 13 \\ +\ 5 \\ \hline \end{array}$
18. $\begin{array}{r} 10 \\ +\ 5 \\ \hline \end{array}$
19. $\begin{array}{r} 4 \\ +\ 5 \\ \hline \end{array}$
20. $\begin{array}{r} 16 \\ -\ 5 \\ \hline \end{array}$

IF87115 *Timed Math Tests*

Subtraction Challenge

Name _____ Date _____

Time _____ Score _____

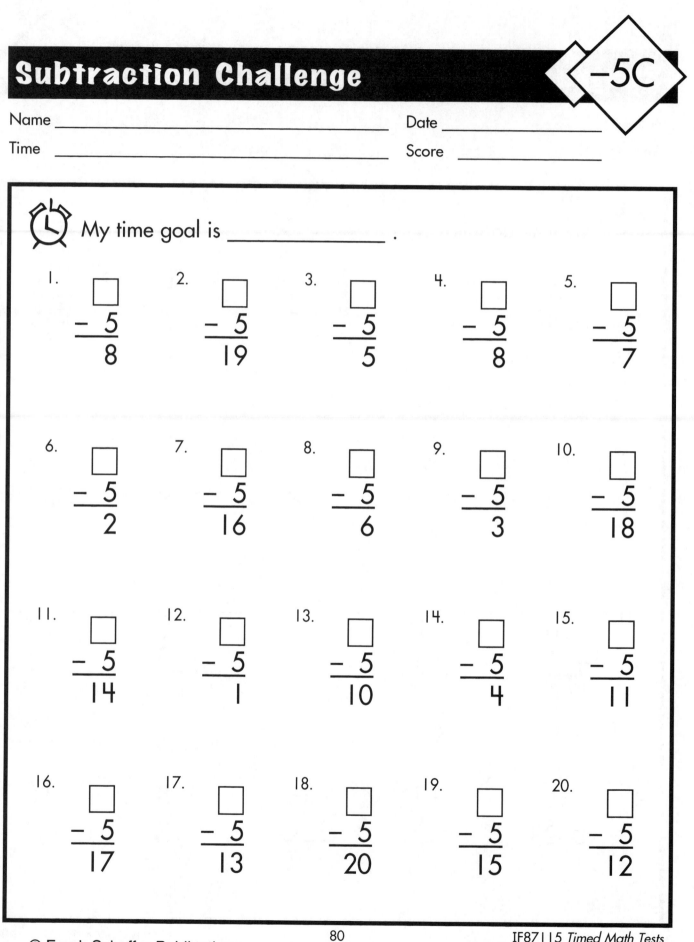

🕐 My time goal is _____ .

1.
$$\begin{array}{r} \square \\ -\ 5 \\ \hline 8 \end{array}$$

2.
$$\begin{array}{r} \square \\ -\ 5 \\ \hline 19 \end{array}$$

3.
$$\begin{array}{r} \square \\ -\ 5 \\ \hline 5 \end{array}$$

4.
$$\begin{array}{r} \square \\ -\ 5 \\ \hline 8 \end{array}$$

5.
$$\begin{array}{r} \square \\ -\ 5 \\ \hline 7 \end{array}$$

6.
$$\begin{array}{r} \square \\ -\ 5 \\ \hline 2 \end{array}$$

7.
$$\begin{array}{r} \square \\ -\ 5 \\ \hline 16 \end{array}$$

8.
$$\begin{array}{r} \square \\ -\ 5 \\ \hline 6 \end{array}$$

9.
$$\begin{array}{r} \square \\ -\ 5 \\ \hline 3 \end{array}$$

10.
$$\begin{array}{r} \square \\ -\ 5 \\ \hline 18 \end{array}$$

11.
$$\begin{array}{r} \square \\ -\ 5 \\ \hline 14 \end{array}$$

12.
$$\begin{array}{r} \square \\ -\ 5 \\ \hline 1 \end{array}$$

13.
$$\begin{array}{r} \square \\ -\ 5 \\ \hline 10 \end{array}$$

14.
$$\begin{array}{r} \square \\ -\ 5 \\ \hline 4 \end{array}$$

15.
$$\begin{array}{r} \square \\ -\ 5 \\ \hline 11 \end{array}$$

16.
$$\begin{array}{r} \square \\ -\ 5 \\ \hline 17 \end{array}$$

17.
$$\begin{array}{r} \square \\ -\ 5 \\ \hline 13 \end{array}$$

18.
$$\begin{array}{r} \square \\ -\ 5 \\ \hline 20 \end{array}$$

19.
$$\begin{array}{r} \square \\ -\ 5 \\ \hline 15 \end{array}$$

20.
$$\begin{array}{r} \square \\ -\ 5 \\ \hline 12 \end{array}$$

IF87115 *Timed Math Tests*

Subtraction Pretest

Name _____   Date _____

Time _____   Score _____

My time goal is _____ .

1. $\begin{array}{r} 8 \\ -6 \\ \hline \end{array}$	2. $\begin{array}{r} 19 \\ -6 \\ \hline \end{array}$	3. $\begin{array}{r} 13 \\ -6 \\ \hline \end{array}$	4. $\begin{array}{r} 10 \\ -6 \\ \hline \end{array}$	5. $\begin{array}{r} 6 \\ -6 \\ \hline \end{array}$
6. $\begin{array}{r} 11 \\ -6 \\ \hline \end{array}$	7. $\begin{array}{r} 14 \\ -6 \\ \hline \end{array}$	8. $\begin{array}{r} 7 \\ -6 \\ \hline \end{array}$	9. $\begin{array}{r} 16 \\ -6 \\ \hline \end{array}$	10. $\begin{array}{r} 9 \\ -6 \\ \hline \end{array}$
11. $\begin{array}{r} 15 \\ -6 \\ \hline \end{array}$	12. $\begin{array}{r} 12 \\ -6 \\ \hline \end{array}$	13. $\begin{array}{r} 9 \\ -6 \\ \hline \end{array}$	14. $\begin{array}{r} 17 \\ -6 \\ \hline \end{array}$	15. $\begin{array}{r} 20 \\ -6 \\ \hline \end{array}$
16. $\begin{array}{r} 14 \\ -6 \\ \hline \end{array}$	17. $\begin{array}{r} 18 \\ -6 \\ \hline \end{array}$	18. $\begin{array}{r} 11 \\ -6 \\ \hline \end{array}$	19. $\begin{array}{r} 19 \\ -6 \\ \hline \end{array}$	20. $\begin{array}{r} 10 \\ -6 \\ \hline \end{array}$

IF87115 *Timed Math Tests*

Subtraction/Addition Practice −6B

Name _____   Date _____

Time _____   Score _____

My time goal is _____ .

1. 12
   + 6

2. 19
   − 6

3. 13
   − 6

4. 7
   + 6

5. 20
   + 6

6. 17
   − 6

7. 18
   + 6

8. 11
   + 6

9. 19
   + 6

10. 16
    − 6

11. 10
    − 6

12. 8
    − 6

13. 14
    − 6

14. 9
    + 6

15. 6
    + 6

16. 8
    + 6

17. 11
    − 6

18. 9
    − 6

19. 20
    − 6

20. 15
    + 6

IF87115 *Timed Math Tests*

Subtraction Challenge

Name _____ Date _____

Time _____ Score _____

My time goal is _____ .

1.
$$\begin{array}{r} \square \\ -\ 6 \\ \hline 15 \end{array}$$

2.
$$\begin{array}{r} \square \\ -\ 6 \\ \hline 12 \end{array}$$

3.
$$\begin{array}{r} \square \\ -\ 6 \\ \hline 20 \end{array}$$

4.
$$\begin{array}{r} \square \\ -\ 6 \\ \hline 13 \end{array}$$

5.
$$\begin{array}{r} \square \\ -\ 6 \\ \hline 17 \end{array}$$

6.
$$\begin{array}{r} \square \\ -\ 6 \\ \hline 11 \end{array}$$

7.
$$\begin{array}{r} \square \\ -\ 6 \\ \hline 10 \end{array}$$

8.
$$\begin{array}{r} \square \\ -\ 6 \\ \hline 4 \end{array}$$

9.
$$\begin{array}{r} \square \\ -\ 6 \\ \hline 1 \end{array}$$

10.
$$\begin{array}{r} \square \\ -\ 6 \\ \hline 14 \end{array}$$

11.
$$\begin{array}{r} \square \\ -\ 6 \\ \hline 18 \end{array}$$

12.
$$\begin{array}{r} \square \\ -\ 6 \\ \hline 3 \end{array}$$

13.
$$\begin{array}{r} \square \\ -\ 6 \\ \hline 6 \end{array}$$

14.
$$\begin{array}{r} \square \\ -\ 6 \\ \hline 16 \end{array}$$

15.
$$\begin{array}{r} \square \\ -\ 6 \\ \hline 2 \end{array}$$

16.
$$\begin{array}{r} \square \\ -\ 6 \\ \hline 7 \end{array}$$

17.
$$\begin{array}{r} \square \\ -\ 6 \\ \hline 8 \end{array}$$

18.
$$\begin{array}{r} \square \\ -\ 6 \\ \hline 5 \end{array}$$

19.
$$\begin{array}{r} \square \\ -\ 6 \\ \hline 19 \end{array}$$

20.
$$\begin{array}{r} \square \\ -\ 6 \\ \hline 9 \end{array}$$

IF87115 *Timed Math Tests*

Subtraction Pretest

Name _____   Date _____

Time _____   Score _____

My time goal is _____ .

1. 15
   − 7

2. 12
   − 7

3. 16
   − 7

4.   9
   − 7

5. 17
   − 7

6. 20
   − 7

7. 14
   − 7

8. 18
   − 7

9. 15
   − 7

10. 24
   − 7

11. 23
   − 7

12. 11
   − 7

13. 8
   − 7

14. 22
   − 7

15. 10
   − 7

16. 13
   − 7

17. 19
   − 7

18. 12
   − 7

19. 18
   − 7

20. 21
   − 7

Subtraction/Addition Practice   −7B

Name _____   Date _____

Time _____   Score _____

My time goal is _____ .

1. $\begin{array}{r} 3 \\ +7 \\ \hline \end{array}$	2. $\begin{array}{r} 17 \\ -7 \\ \hline \end{array}$	3. $\begin{array}{r} 10 \\ -7 \\ \hline \end{array}$	4. $\begin{array}{r} 14 \\ +7 \\ \hline \end{array}$	5. $\begin{array}{r} 9 \\ -7 \\ \hline \end{array}$
6. $\begin{array}{r} 6 \\ +7 \\ \hline \end{array}$	7. $\begin{array}{r} 20 \\ +7 \\ \hline \end{array}$	8. $\begin{array}{r} 7 \\ +7 \\ \hline \end{array}$	9. $\begin{array}{r} 11 \\ +7 \\ \hline \end{array}$	10. $\begin{array}{r} 21 \\ -7 \\ \hline \end{array}$
11. $\begin{array}{r} 18 \\ -7 \\ \hline \end{array}$	12. $\begin{array}{r} 11 \\ -7 \\ \hline \end{array}$	13. $\begin{array}{r} 2 \\ +7 \\ \hline \end{array}$	14. $\begin{array}{r} 19 \\ -7 \\ \hline \end{array}$	15. $\begin{array}{r} 12 \\ -7 \\ \hline \end{array}$
16. $\begin{array}{r} 15 \\ -7 \\ \hline \end{array}$	17. $\begin{array}{r} 13 \\ +7 \\ \hline \end{array}$	18. $\begin{array}{r} 23 \\ -7 \\ \hline \end{array}$	19. $\begin{array}{r} 4 \\ +7 \\ \hline \end{array}$	20. $\begin{array}{r} 16 \\ +7 \\ \hline \end{array}$

IF87115 *Timed Math Tests*

Subtraction Challenge

Name _____   Date _____

Time _____   Score _____

🕐 My time goal is _____ .

1. $\square - 7 = 9$

2. $\square - 7 = 19$

3. $\square - 7 = 15$

4. $\square - 7 = 8$

5. $\square - 7 = 17$

6. $\square - 7 = 2$

7. $\square - 7 = 16$

8. $\square - 7 = 6$

9. $\square - 7 = 23$

10. $\square - 7 = 18$

11. $\square - 7 = 14$

12. $\square - 7 = 21$

13. $\square - 7 = 10$

14. $\square - 7 = 4$

15. $\square - 7 = 11$

16. $\square - 7 = 7$

17. $\square - 7 = 13$

18. $\square - 7 = 20$

19. $\square - 7 = 22$

20. $\square - 7 = 12$

IF87115 *Timed Math Tests*

Subtraction Pretest

Name _____   Date _____

Time _____   Score _____

🕐 My time goal is _____ .

1.
$$\begin{array}{r} 25 \\ -\ 8 \\ \hline \end{array}$$

2.
$$\begin{array}{r} 19 \\ -\ 8 \\ \hline \end{array}$$

3.
$$\begin{array}{r} 13 \\ -\ 8 \\ \hline \end{array}$$

4.
$$\begin{array}{r} 10 \\ -\ 8 \\ \hline \end{array}$$

5.
$$\begin{array}{r} 22 \\ -\ 8 \\ \hline \end{array}$$

6.
$$\begin{array}{r} 11 \\ -\ 8 \\ \hline \end{array}$$

7.
$$\begin{array}{r} 24 \\ -\ 8 \\ \hline \end{array}$$

8.
$$\begin{array}{r} 26 \\ -\ 8 \\ \hline \end{array}$$

9.
$$\begin{array}{r} 16 \\ -\ 8 \\ \hline \end{array}$$

10.
$$\begin{array}{r} 23 \\ -\ 8 \\ \hline \end{array}$$

11.
$$\begin{array}{r} 15 \\ -\ 8 \\ \hline \end{array}$$

12.
$$\begin{array}{r} 12 \\ -\ 8 \\ \hline \end{array}$$

13.
$$\begin{array}{r} 9 \\ -\ 8 \\ \hline \end{array}$$

14.
$$\begin{array}{r} 17 \\ -\ 8 \\ \hline \end{array}$$

15.
$$\begin{array}{r} 20 \\ -\ 8 \\ \hline \end{array}$$

16.
$$\begin{array}{r} 14 \\ -\ 8 \\ \hline \end{array}$$

17.
$$\begin{array}{r} 18 \\ -\ 8 \\ \hline \end{array}$$

18.
$$\begin{array}{r} 11 \\ -\ 8 \\ \hline \end{array}$$

19.
$$\begin{array}{r} 19 \\ -\ 8 \\ \hline \end{array}$$

20.
$$\begin{array}{r} 21 \\ -\ 8 \\ \hline \end{array}$$

IF87115 *Timed Math Tests*

Subtraction/Addition Practice −8B

Name _____   Date _____

Time _____   Score _____

My time goal is _____ .

1. $\begin{array}{r} 8 \\ +\ 8 \\ \hline \end{array}$	2. $\begin{array}{r} 11 \\ +\ 8 \\ \hline \end{array}$	3. $\begin{array}{r} 18 \\ -\ 8 \\ \hline \end{array}$	4. $\begin{array}{r} 5 \\ +\ 8 \\ \hline \end{array}$	5. $\begin{array}{r} 20 \\ -\ 8 \\ \hline \end{array}$
6. $\begin{array}{r} 19 \\ +\ 8 \\ \hline \end{array}$	7. $\begin{array}{r} 21 \\ -\ 8 \\ \hline \end{array}$	8. $\begin{array}{r} 9 \\ +\ 8 \\ \hline \end{array}$	9. $\begin{array}{r} 17 \\ -\ 8 \\ \hline \end{array}$	10. $\begin{array}{r} 10 \\ -\ 8 \\ \hline \end{array}$
11. $\begin{array}{r} 18 \\ -\ 8 \\ \hline \end{array}$	12. $\begin{array}{r} 16 \\ -\ 8 \\ \hline \end{array}$	13. $\begin{array}{r} 13 \\ -\ 8 \\ \hline \end{array}$	14. $\begin{array}{r} 20 \\ +\ 8 \\ \hline \end{array}$	15. $\begin{array}{r} 14 \\ +\ 8 \\ \hline \end{array}$
16. $\begin{array}{r} 19 \\ -\ 8 \\ \hline \end{array}$	17. $\begin{array}{r} 14 \\ -\ 8 \\ \hline \end{array}$	18. $\begin{array}{r} 6 \\ +\ 8 \\ \hline \end{array}$	19. $\begin{array}{r} 13 \\ +\ 8 \\ \hline \end{array}$	20. $\begin{array}{r} 11 \\ -\ 8 \\ \hline \end{array}$

IF87115 *Timed Math Tests*

Subtraction Challenge

Name _____   Date _____

Time _____   Score _____

⏰ My time goal is _____ .

1. $\square$ $-\ 8$ ___ 15	2. $\square$ $-\ 8$ ___ 12	3. $\square$ $-\ 8$ ___ 20	4. $\square$ $-\ 8$ ___ 13	5. $\square$ $-\ 8$ ___ 17
6. $\square$ $-\ 8$ ___ 11	7. $\square$ $-\ 8$ ___ 10	8. $\square$ $-\ 8$ ___ 4	9. $\square$ $-\ 8$ ___ 1	10. $\square$ $-\ 8$ ___ 14
11. $\square$ $-\ 8$ ___ 18	12. $\square$ $-\ 8$ ___ 3	13. $\square$ $-\ 8$ ___ 6	14. $\square$ $-\ 8$ ___ 16	15. $\square$ $-\ 8$ ___ 2
16. $\square$ $-\ 8$ ___ 7	17. $\square$ $-\ 8$ ___ 8	18. $\square$ $-\ 8$ ___ 5	19. $\square$ $-\ 8$ ___ 19	20. $\square$ $-\ 8$ ___ 9

IF87115 *Timed Math Tests*

Subtraction Pretest

Name _____   Date _____

Time _____   Score _____

🕐 My time goal is _____ .

1. $\begin{array}{r} 15 \\ -\ 9 \\ \hline \end{array}$
2. $\begin{array}{r} 12 \\ -\ 9 \\ \hline \end{array}$
3. $\begin{array}{r} 21 \\ -\ 9 \\ \hline \end{array}$
4. $\begin{array}{r} 9 \\ -\ 9 \\ \hline \end{array}$
5. $\begin{array}{r} 17 \\ -\ 9 \\ \hline \end{array}$

6. $\begin{array}{r} 20 \\ -\ 9 \\ \hline \end{array}$
7. $\begin{array}{r} 14 \\ -\ 9 \\ \hline \end{array}$
8. $\begin{array}{r} 18 \\ -\ 9 \\ \hline \end{array}$
9. $\begin{array}{r} 23 \\ -\ 9 \\ \hline \end{array}$
10. $\begin{array}{r} 25 \\ -\ 9 \\ \hline \end{array}$

11. $\begin{array}{r} 16 \\ -\ 9 \\ \hline \end{array}$
12. $\begin{array}{r} 24 \\ -\ 9 \\ \hline \end{array}$
13. $\begin{array}{r} 11 \\ -\ 9 \\ \hline \end{array}$
14. $\begin{array}{r} 22 \\ -\ 9 \\ \hline \end{array}$
15. $\begin{array}{r} 26 \\ -\ 9 \\ \hline \end{array}$

16. $\begin{array}{r} 10 \\ -\ 9 \\ \hline \end{array}$
17. $\begin{array}{r} 13 \\ -\ 9 \\ \hline \end{array}$
18. $\begin{array}{r} 19 \\ -\ 9 \\ \hline \end{array}$
19. $\begin{array}{r} 12 \\ -\ 9 \\ \hline \end{array}$
20. $\begin{array}{r} 18 \\ -\ 9 \\ \hline \end{array}$

IF87115 *Timed Math Tests*

Subtraction/Addition Practice   −9B

Name _____   Date _____

Time _____   Score _____

My time goal is _____ .

1. $\begin{array}{r} 3 \\ +\ 9 \\ \hline \end{array}$	2. $\begin{array}{r} 17 \\ -\ 9 \\ \hline \end{array}$	3. $\begin{array}{r} 10 \\ -\ 9 \\ \hline \end{array}$	4. $\begin{array}{r} 14 \\ +\ 9 \\ \hline \end{array}$	5. $\begin{array}{r} 5 \\ +\ 9 \\ \hline \end{array}$
6. $\begin{array}{r} 13 \\ -\ 9 \\ \hline \end{array}$	7. $\begin{array}{r} 20 \\ +\ 9 \\ \hline \end{array}$	8. $\begin{array}{r} 17 \\ -\ 9 \\ \hline \end{array}$	9. $\begin{array}{r} 11 \\ +\ 9 \\ \hline \end{array}$	10. $\begin{array}{r} 21 \\ -\ 9 \\ \hline \end{array}$
11. $\begin{array}{r} 18 \\ -\ 9 \\ \hline \end{array}$	12. $\begin{array}{r} 11 \\ -\ 9 \\ \hline \end{array}$	13. $\begin{array}{r} 12 \\ +\ 9 \\ \hline \end{array}$	14. $\begin{array}{r} 19 \\ -\ 9 \\ \hline \end{array}$	15. $\begin{array}{r} 12 \\ -\ 9 \\ \hline \end{array}$
16. $\begin{array}{r} 15 \\ -\ 9 \\ \hline \end{array}$	17. $\begin{array}{r} 13 \\ +\ 9 \\ \hline \end{array}$	18. $\begin{array}{r} 14 \\ -\ 9 \\ \hline \end{array}$	19. $\begin{array}{r} 4 \\ +\ 9 \\ \hline \end{array}$	20. $\begin{array}{r} 16 \\ -\ 9 \\ \hline \end{array}$

IF87115 *Timed Math Tests*

Subtraction Challenge

Name _____   Date _____

Time _____   Score _____

🕐 My time goal is _____ .

1.
$$\begin{array}{r} \square \\ -\ 9 \\ \hline 9 \end{array}$$

2.
$$\begin{array}{r} \square \\ -\ 9 \\ \hline 19 \end{array}$$

3.
$$\begin{array}{r} \square \\ -\ 9 \\ \hline 5 \end{array}$$

4.
$$\begin{array}{r} \square \\ -\ 9 \\ \hline 8 \end{array}$$

5.
$$\begin{array}{r} \square \\ -\ 9 \\ \hline 7 \end{array}$$

6.
$$\begin{array}{r} \square \\ -\ 9 \\ \hline 2 \end{array}$$

7.
$$\begin{array}{r} \square \\ -\ 9 \\ \hline 16 \end{array}$$

8.
$$\begin{array}{r} \square \\ -\ 9 \\ \hline 6 \end{array}$$

9.
$$\begin{array}{r} \square \\ -\ 9 \\ \hline 3 \end{array}$$

10.
$$\begin{array}{r} \square \\ -\ 9 \\ \hline 18 \end{array}$$

11.
$$\begin{array}{r} \square \\ -\ 9 \\ \hline 14 \end{array}$$

12.
$$\begin{array}{r} \square \\ -\ 9 \\ \hline 1 \end{array}$$

13.
$$\begin{array}{r} \square \\ -\ 9 \\ \hline 10 \end{array}$$

14.
$$\begin{array}{r} \square \\ -\ 9 \\ \hline 4 \end{array}$$

15.
$$\begin{array}{r} \square \\ -\ 9 \\ \hline 11 \end{array}$$

16.
$$\begin{array}{r} \square \\ -\ 9 \\ \hline 17 \end{array}$$

17.
$$\begin{array}{r} \square \\ -\ 9 \\ \hline 13 \end{array}$$

18.
$$\begin{array}{r} \square \\ -\ 9 \\ \hline 20 \end{array}$$

19.
$$\begin{array}{r} \square \\ -\ 9 \\ \hline 15 \end{array}$$

20.
$$\begin{array}{r} \square \\ -\ 9 \\ \hline 12 \end{array}$$

IF87115 *Timed Math Tests*

Subtraction Pretest

Name _____ Date _____

Time _____ Score _____

🕐 My time goal is _____ .

1.   15
   − 10

2.   12
   − 10

3.   26
   − 10

4.   18
   − 10

5.   24
   − 10

6.   21
   − 10

7.   17
   − 10

8.   23
   − 10

9.   20
   − 10

10. 14
   − 10

11. 13
   − 10

12. 16
   − 10

13. 27
   − 10

14. 11
   − 10

15. 28
   − 10

16. 25
   − 10

17. 10
   − 10

18. 13
   − 10

19. 19
   − 10

20. 22
   − 10

IF87115 *Timed Math Tests*

Subtraction/Addition Practice
−10B

Name _____ Date _____

Time _____ Score _____

My time goal is _____ .

1.
$$19 - 10$$

2.
$$3 + 10$$

3.
$$16 - 10$$

4.
$$13 + 10$$

5.
$$14 - 10$$

6.
$$17 - 10$$

7.
$$18 + 10$$

8.
$$20 - 10$$

9.
$$4 + 10$$

10.
$$19 + 10$$

11.
$$15 - 10$$

12.
$$11 + 10$$

13.
$$18 - 10$$

14.
$$21 - 10$$

15.
$$6 + 10$$

16.
$$10 + 10$$

17.
$$21 + 10$$

18.
$$7 + 10$$

19.
$$12 - 10$$

20.
$$23 - 10$$

IF87115 *Timed Math Tests*

Subtraction Challenge

Name _____   Date _____

Time _____   Score _____

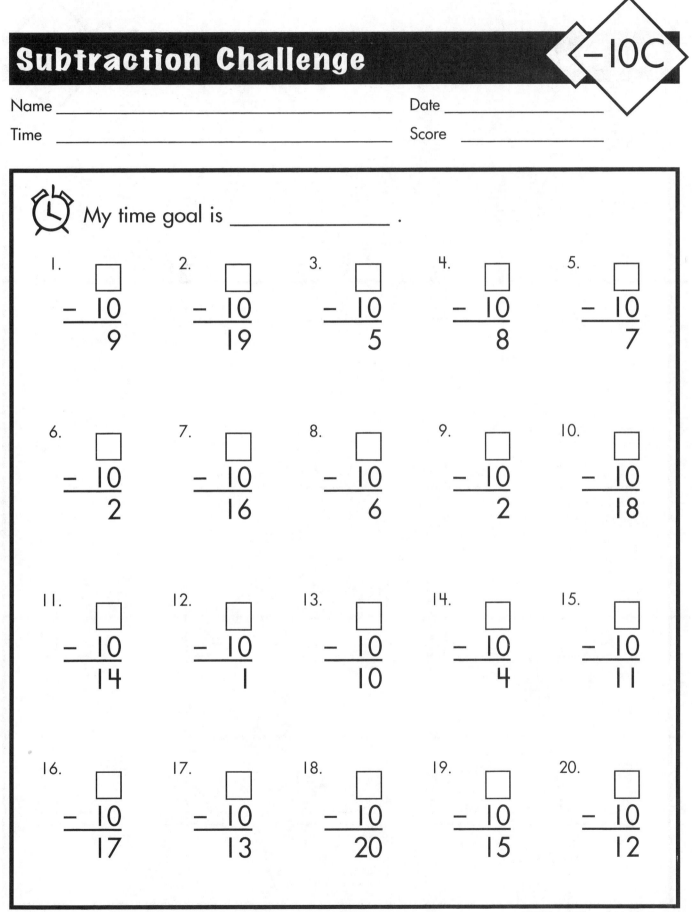

My time goal is _____ .

1.
$$\begin{array}{r} \square \\ -\ 10 \\ \hline 9 \end{array}$$

2.
$$\begin{array}{r} \square \\ -\ 10 \\ \hline 19 \end{array}$$

3.
$$\begin{array}{r} \square \\ -\ 10 \\ \hline 5 \end{array}$$

4.
$$\begin{array}{r} \square \\ -\ 10 \\ \hline 8 \end{array}$$

5.
$$\begin{array}{r} \square \\ -\ 10 \\ \hline 7 \end{array}$$

6.
$$\begin{array}{r} \square \\ -\ 10 \\ \hline 2 \end{array}$$

7.
$$\begin{array}{r} \square \\ -\ 10 \\ \hline 16 \end{array}$$

8.
$$\begin{array}{r} \square \\ -\ 10 \\ \hline 6 \end{array}$$

9.
$$\begin{array}{r} \square \\ -\ 10 \\ \hline 2 \end{array}$$

10.
$$\begin{array}{r} \square \\ -\ 10 \\ \hline 18 \end{array}$$

11.
$$\begin{array}{r} \square \\ -\ 10 \\ \hline 14 \end{array}$$

12.
$$\begin{array}{r} \square \\ -\ 10 \\ \hline 1 \end{array}$$

13.
$$\begin{array}{r} \square \\ -\ 10 \\ \hline 10 \end{array}$$

14.
$$\begin{array}{r} \square \\ -\ 10 \\ \hline 4 \end{array}$$

15.
$$\begin{array}{r} \square \\ -\ 10 \\ \hline 11 \end{array}$$

16.
$$\begin{array}{r} \square \\ -\ 10 \\ \hline 17 \end{array}$$

17.
$$\begin{array}{r} \square \\ -\ 10 \\ \hline 13 \end{array}$$

18.
$$\begin{array}{r} \square \\ -\ 10 \\ \hline 20 \end{array}$$

19.
$$\begin{array}{r} \square \\ -\ 10 \\ \hline 15 \end{array}$$

20.
$$\begin{array}{r} \square \\ -\ 10 \\ \hline 12 \end{array}$$

Name _____ Date _____

Time _____ Score _____

⏰ My time goal is _____ .

1. 28 – 11	2. 19 – 11	3. 13 – 11	4. 21 – 11	5. 26 – 11
6. 11 – 11	7. 14 – 11	8. 27 – 11	9. 16 – 11	10. 25 – 11
11. 15 – 11	12. 22 – 11	13. 29 – 11	14. 17 – 11	15. 20 – 11
16. 24 – 11	17. 18 – 11	18. 30 – 11	19. 12 – 11	20. 23 – 11

IF87115 *Timed Math Tests*

Subtraction/Addition Practice

Name _____   Date _____

Time _____   Score _____

🕐 My time goal is _____ .

1.
$$\begin{array}{r} 8 \\ +\ 11 \\ \hline \end{array}$$

2.
$$\begin{array}{r} 11 \\ +\ 11 \\ \hline \end{array}$$

3.
$$\begin{array}{r} 18 \\ -\ 11 \\ \hline \end{array}$$

4.
$$\begin{array}{r} 20 \\ -\ 11 \\ \hline \end{array}$$

5.
$$\begin{array}{r} 5 \\ +\ 11 \\ \hline \end{array}$$

6.
$$\begin{array}{r} 23 \\ -\ 11 \\ \hline \end{array}$$

7.
$$\begin{array}{r} 18 \\ +\ 11 \\ \hline \end{array}$$

8.
$$\begin{array}{r} 26 \\ -\ 11 \\ \hline \end{array}$$

9.
$$\begin{array}{r} 17 \\ -\ 11 \\ \hline \end{array}$$

10.
$$\begin{array}{r} 19 \\ -\ 11 \\ \hline \end{array}$$

11.
$$\begin{array}{r} 18 \\ -\ 11 \\ \hline \end{array}$$

12.
$$\begin{array}{r} 16 \\ -\ 11 \\ \hline \end{array}$$

13.
$$\begin{array}{r} 13 \\ -\ 11 \\ \hline \end{array}$$

14.
$$\begin{array}{r} 19 \\ +\ 11 \\ \hline \end{array}$$

15.
$$\begin{array}{r} 4 \\ +\ 11 \\ \hline \end{array}$$

16.
$$\begin{array}{r} 24 \\ -\ 11 \\ \hline \end{array}$$

17.
$$\begin{array}{r} 14 \\ -\ 11 \\ \hline \end{array}$$

18.
$$\begin{array}{r} 6 \\ +\ 11 \\ \hline \end{array}$$

19.
$$\begin{array}{r} 13 \\ +\ 11 \\ \hline \end{array}$$

20.
$$\begin{array}{r} 21 \\ -\ 11 \\ \hline \end{array}$$

IF87115 *Timed Math Tests*

Subtraction Challenge

Name _____   Date _____

Time _____   Score _____

🕐 My time goal is _____ .

1. □
    − 11
    ‾‾‾‾
    15

2. □
    − 11
    ‾‾‾‾
    12

3. □
    − 11
    ‾‾‾‾
    20

4. □
    − 11
    ‾‾‾‾
    13

5. □
    − 11
    ‾‾‾‾
    17

6. □
    − 11
    ‾‾‾‾
    11

7. □
    − 11
    ‾‾‾‾
    10

8. □
    − 11
    ‾‾‾‾
    4

9. □
    − 11
    ‾‾‾‾
    1

10. □
    − 11
    ‾‾‾‾
    14

11. □
    − 11
    ‾‾‾‾
    18

12. □
    − 11
    ‾‾‾‾
    3

13. □
    − 11
    ‾‾‾‾
    6

14. □
    − 11
    ‾‾‾‾
    16

15. □
    − 11
    ‾‾‾‾
    2

16. □
    − 11
    ‾‾‾‾
    7

17. □
    − 11
    ‾‾‾‾
    8

18. □
    − 11
    ‾‾‾‾
    5

19. □
    − 11
    ‾‾‾‾
    19

20. □
    − 11
    ‾‾‾‾
    9

IF87115 *Timed Math Tests*

Subtraction Pretest

Name _____   Date _____

Time _____   Score _____

🕐 My time goal is _____ .

1. 15
   − 12

2. 12
   − 12

3. 16
   − 12

4. 29
   − 12

5. 17
   − 12

6. 20
   − 12

7. 14
   − 12

8. 18
   − 12

9. 25
   − 12

10. 21
    − 12

11. 23
    − 12

12. 26
    − 12

13. 30
    − 12

14. 22
    − 12

15. 27
    − 12

16. 13
    − 12

17. 19
    − 12

18. 28
    − 12

19. 18
    − 12

20. 24
    − 12

Subtraction/Addition Practice ⟨–12B⟩

Name _____   Date _____

Time _____   Score _____

🕐 My time goal is _____ .

1.
$\begin{array}{r} 3 \\ +\ 12 \\ \hline \end{array}$

2.
$\begin{array}{r} 17 \\ -\ 12 \\ \hline \end{array}$

3.
$\begin{array}{r} 25 \\ -\ 12 \\ \hline \end{array}$

4.
$\begin{array}{r} 14 \\ +\ 12 \\ \hline \end{array}$

5.
$\begin{array}{r} 22 \\ -\ 12 \\ \hline \end{array}$

6.
$\begin{array}{r} 6 \\ +\ 12 \\ \hline \end{array}$

7.
$\begin{array}{r} 20 \\ -\ 12 \\ \hline \end{array}$

8.
$\begin{array}{r} 7 \\ +\ 12 \\ \hline \end{array}$

9.
$\begin{array}{r} 11 \\ +\ 12 \\ \hline \end{array}$

10.
$\begin{array}{r} 21 \\ -\ 12 \\ \hline \end{array}$

11.
$\begin{array}{r} 18 \\ -\ 12 \\ \hline \end{array}$

12.
$\begin{array}{r} 11 \\ +\ 12 \\ \hline \end{array}$

13.
$\begin{array}{r} 2 \\ +\ 12 \\ \hline \end{array}$

14.
$\begin{array}{r} 19 \\ -\ 12 \\ \hline \end{array}$

15.
$\begin{array}{r} 12 \\ +\ 12 \\ \hline \end{array}$

16.
$\begin{array}{r} 15 \\ -\ 12 \\ \hline \end{array}$

17.
$\begin{array}{r} 13 \\ +\ 12 \\ \hline \end{array}$

18.
$\begin{array}{r} 23 \\ -\ 12 \\ \hline \end{array}$

19.
$\begin{array}{r} 4 \\ +\ 12 \\ \hline \end{array}$

20.
$\begin{array}{r} 16 \\ -\ 12 \\ \hline \end{array}$

       IF87115 *Timed Math Tests*

Subtraction Challenge

Name _____   Date _____

Time _____   Score _____

⏰ My time goal is _____ .

1. ☐
   − 12
   ___
    9

2. ☐
   − 12
   ___
   19

3. ☐
   − 12
   ___
   15

4. ☐
   − 12
   ___
    8

5. ☐
   − 12
   ___
   17

6. ☐
   − 12
   ___
    2

7. ☐
   − 12
   ___
   16

8. ☐
   − 12
   ___
    6

9. ☐
   − 12
   ___
   23

10. ☐
   − 12
   ___
   18

11. ☐
   − 12
   ___
   14

12. ☐
   − 12
   ___
   21

13. ☐
   − 12
   ___
   10

14. ☐
   − 12
   ___
    4

15. ☐
   − 12
   ___
   11

16. ☐
   − 12
   ___
    7

17. ☐
   − 12
   ___
   13

18. ☐
   − 12
   ___
   20

19. ☐
   − 12
   ___
   22

20. ☐
   − 12
   ___
   12

IF87115 *Timed Math Tests*

Subtraction Pretest

Name _____   Date _____

Time _____   Score _____

🕐 My time goal is _____ .

1. 24
  − 13

2. 19
  − 13

3. 13
  − 13

4. 26
  − 13

5. 22
  − 13

6. 30
  − 13

7. 25
  − 13

8. 29
  − 13

9. 16
  − 13

10. 23
   − 13

11. 15
   − 13

12. 31
   − 13

13. 28
   − 13

14. 17
   − 13

15. 20
   − 13

16. 14
   − 13

17. 18
   − 13

18. 27
   − 13

19. 32
   − 13

20. 21
   − 13

Subtraction/Addition Practice ⟨−13B⟩

Name _____ Date _____

Time _____ Score _____

🕐 My time goal is _____ .

1. $\begin{array}{r} 8 \\ +\ 13 \\ \hline \end{array}$	2. $\begin{array}{r} 11 \\ +\ 13 \\ \hline \end{array}$	3. $\begin{array}{r} 18 \\ -\ 13 \\ \hline \end{array}$	4. $\begin{array}{r} 5 \\ +\ 13 \\ \hline \end{array}$	5. $\begin{array}{r} 20 \\ -\ 13 \\ \hline \end{array}$
6. $\begin{array}{r} 19 \\ +\ 13 \\ \hline \end{array}$	7. $\begin{array}{r} 21 \\ -\ 13 \\ \hline \end{array}$	8. $\begin{array}{r} 9 \\ +\ 13 \\ \hline \end{array}$	9. $\begin{array}{r} 17 \\ -\ 13 \\ \hline \end{array}$	10. $\begin{array}{r} 10 \\ +\ 13 \\ \hline \end{array}$
11. $\begin{array}{r} 28 \\ -\ 13 \\ \hline \end{array}$	12. $\begin{array}{r} 16 \\ -\ 13 \\ \hline \end{array}$	13. $\begin{array}{r} 33 \\ -\ 13 \\ \hline \end{array}$	14. $\begin{array}{r} 20 \\ +\ 13 \\ \hline \end{array}$	15. $\begin{array}{r} 14 \\ +\ 13 \\ \hline \end{array}$
16. $\begin{array}{r} 29 \\ -\ 13 \\ \hline \end{array}$	17. $\begin{array}{r} 24 \\ -\ 13 \\ \hline \end{array}$	18. $\begin{array}{r} 6 \\ +\ 13 \\ \hline \end{array}$	19. $\begin{array}{r} 13 \\ +\ 13 \\ \hline \end{array}$	20. $\begin{array}{r} 22 \\ -\ 13 \\ \hline \end{array}$

IF87115 *Timed Math Tests*

Subtraction Challenge

Name _____   Date _____

Time _____   Score _____

🕐 My time goal is _____ .

1.
$$\begin{array}{r} \square \\ -\ 13 \\ \hline 15 \end{array}$$

2.
$$\begin{array}{r} \square \\ -\ 13 \\ \hline 12 \end{array}$$

3.
$$\begin{array}{r} \square \\ -\ 13 \\ \hline 20 \end{array}$$

4.
$$\begin{array}{r} \square \\ -\ 13 \\ \hline 13 \end{array}$$

5.
$$\begin{array}{r} \square \\ -\ 13 \\ \hline 17 \end{array}$$

6.
$$\begin{array}{r} \square \\ -\ 13 \\ \hline 11 \end{array}$$

7.
$$\begin{array}{r} \square \\ -\ 13 \\ \hline 10 \end{array}$$

8.
$$\begin{array}{r} \square \\ -\ 13 \\ \hline 4 \end{array}$$

9.
$$\begin{array}{r} \square \\ -\ 13 \\ \hline 1 \end{array}$$

10.
$$\begin{array}{r} \square \\ -\ 13 \\ \hline 14 \end{array}$$

11.
$$\begin{array}{r} \square \\ -\ 13 \\ \hline 18 \end{array}$$

12.
$$\begin{array}{r} \square \\ -\ 13 \\ \hline 3 \end{array}$$

13.
$$\begin{array}{r} \square \\ -\ 13 \\ \hline 6 \end{array}$$

14.
$$\begin{array}{r} \square \\ -\ 13 \\ \hline 16 \end{array}$$

15.
$$\begin{array}{r} \square \\ -\ 13 \\ \hline 2 \end{array}$$

16.
$$\begin{array}{r} \square \\ -\ 13 \\ \hline 7 \end{array}$$

17.
$$\begin{array}{r} \square \\ -\ 13 \\ \hline 8 \end{array}$$

18.
$$\begin{array}{r} \square \\ -\ 13 \\ \hline 5 \end{array}$$

19.
$$\begin{array}{r} \square \\ -\ 13 \\ \hline 19 \end{array}$$

20.
$$\begin{array}{r} \square \\ -\ 13 \\ \hline 9 \end{array}$$

Subtraction Pretest

Name _____ Date _____

Time _____ Score _____

⏰ My time goal is _____ .

1. 15 − 14	2. 27 − 14	3. 21 − 14	4. 29 − 14	5. 17 − 14
6. 20 − 14	7. 14 − 14	8. 18 − 14	9. 23 − 14	10. 25 − 14
11. 32 − 14	12. 24 − 14	13. 28 − 14	14. 22 − 14	15. 26 − 14
16. 30 − 14	17. 18 − 14	18. 19 − 14	19. 16 − 14	20. 31 − 14

Subtraction/Addition Practice   −14B

Name _____   Date _____

Time _____   Score _____

My time goal is _____ .

1.
$$3$$
$$+\ 14$$

2.
$$17$$
$$-\ 14$$

3.
$$20$$
$$-\ 14$$

4.
$$14$$
$$+\ 14$$

5.
$$5$$
$$+\ 14$$

6.
$$23$$
$$-\ 14$$

7.
$$20$$
$$+\ 14$$

8.
$$17$$
$$-\ 14$$

9.
$$11$$
$$+\ 14$$

10.
$$21$$
$$-\ 14$$

11.
$$18$$
$$-\ 14$$

12.
$$22$$
$$-\ 14$$

13.
$$12$$
$$+\ 14$$

14.
$$19$$
$$-\ 14$$

15.
$$24$$
$$-\ 14$$

16.
$$15$$
$$-\ 14$$

17.
$$13$$
$$+\ 14$$

18.
$$26$$
$$-\ 14$$

19.
$$4$$
$$+\ 14$$

20.
$$30$$
$$-\ 14$$

IF87115 *Timed Math Tests*

Subtraction Challenge

Name _____ Date _____

Time _____ Score _____

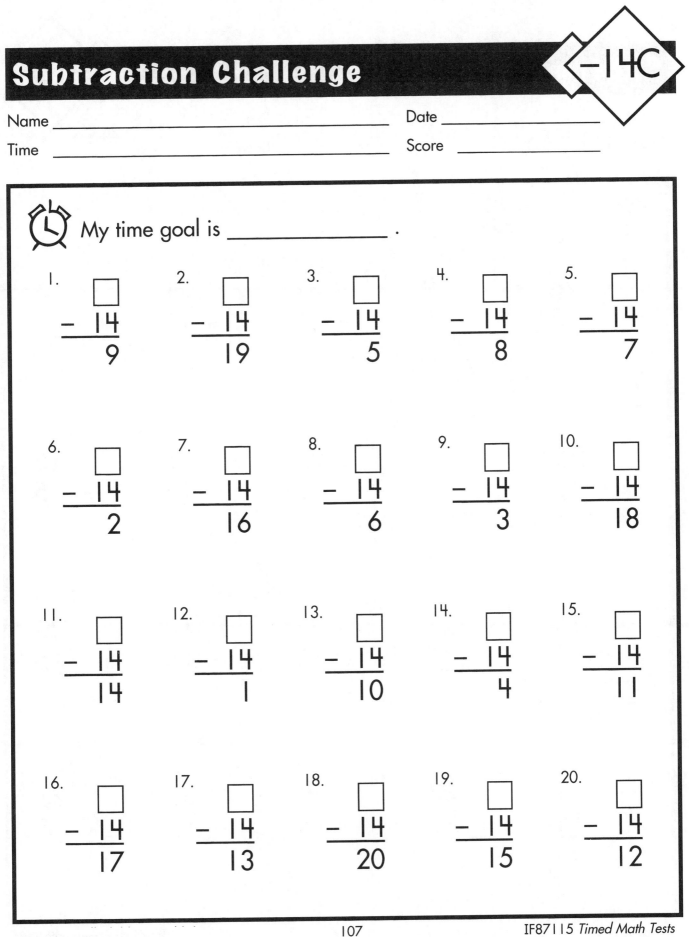

My time goal is _____ .

1.
☐
− 14
9

2.
☐
− 14
19

3.
☐
− 14
5

4.
☐
− 14
8

5.
☐
− 14
7

6.
☐
− 14
2

7.
☐
− 14
16

8.
☐
− 14
6

9.
☐
− 14
3

10.
☐
− 14
18

11.
☐
− 14
14

12.
☐
− 14
1

13.
☐
− 14
10

14.
☐
− 14
4

15.
☐
− 14
11

16.
☐
− 14
17

17.
☐
− 14
13

18.
☐
− 14
20

19.
☐
− 14
15

20.
☐
− 14
12

IF87115 *Timed Math Tests*

Subtraction Pretest

Name _____ Date _____

Time _____ Score _____

My time goal is _____ .

1.
$$28$$
$$- 15$$

2.
$$19$$
$$- 15$$

3.
$$31$$
$$- 15$$

4.
$$21$$
$$- 15$$

5.
$$26$$
$$- 15$$

6.
$$18$$
$$- 15$$

7.
$$34$$
$$- 15$$

8.
$$27$$
$$- 15$$

9.
$$16$$
$$- 15$$

10.
$$25$$
$$- 15$$

11.
$$15$$
$$- 15$$

12.
$$22$$
$$- 15$$

13.
$$29$$
$$- 15$$

14.
$$17$$
$$- 15$$

15.
$$20$$
$$- 15$$

16.
$$24$$
$$- 15$$

17.
$$33$$
$$- 15$$

18.
$$30$$
$$- 15$$

19.
$$35$$
$$- 15$$

20.
$$23$$
$$- 15$$

Subtraction/Addition Practice −15B

Name _____ Date _____

Time _____ Score _____

My time goal is _____ .

1. $\begin{array}{r} 8 \\ + 15 \\ \hline \end{array}$
2. $\begin{array}{r} 11 \\ + 15 \\ \hline \end{array}$
3. $\begin{array}{r} 18 \\ - 15 \\ \hline \end{array}$
4. $\begin{array}{r} 20 \\ - 15 \\ \hline \end{array}$
5. $\begin{array}{r} 5 \\ + 15 \\ \hline \end{array}$

6. $\begin{array}{r} 23 \\ - 15 \\ \hline \end{array}$
7. $\begin{array}{r} 15 \\ - 15 \\ \hline \end{array}$
8. $\begin{array}{r} 26 \\ - 15 \\ \hline \end{array}$
9. $\begin{array}{r} 17 \\ - 15 \\ \hline \end{array}$
10. $\begin{array}{r} 19 \\ - 15 \\ \hline \end{array}$

11. $\begin{array}{r} 28 \\ - 15 \\ \hline \end{array}$
12. $\begin{array}{r} 16 \\ - 15 \\ \hline \end{array}$
13. $\begin{array}{r} 25 \\ - 15 \\ \hline \end{array}$
14. $\begin{array}{r} 19 \\ - 15 \\ \hline \end{array}$
15. $\begin{array}{r} 4 \\ + 15 \\ \hline \end{array}$

16. $\begin{array}{r} 24 \\ - 15 \\ \hline \end{array}$
17. $\begin{array}{r} 21 \\ - 15 \\ \hline \end{array}$
18. $\begin{array}{r} 6 \\ + 15 \\ \hline \end{array}$
19. $\begin{array}{r} 13 \\ + 15 \\ \hline \end{array}$
20. $\begin{array}{r} 22 \\ - 15 \\ \hline \end{array}$

IF87115 *Timed Math Tests*

Subtraction Challenge

Name _____   Date _____

Time _____   Score _____

🕐 My time goal is _____ .

1.
$$\begin{array}{r} \square \\ -\ 15 \\ \hline 15 \end{array}$$

2.
$$\begin{array}{r} \square \\ -\ 15 \\ \hline 12 \end{array}$$

3.
$$\begin{array}{r} \square \\ -\ 15 \\ \hline 20 \end{array}$$

4.
$$\begin{array}{r} \square \\ -\ 15 \\ \hline 13 \end{array}$$

5.
$$\begin{array}{r} \square \\ -\ 15 \\ \hline 17 \end{array}$$

6.
$$\begin{array}{r} \square \\ -\ 15 \\ \hline 11 \end{array}$$

7.
$$\begin{array}{r} \square \\ -\ 15 \\ \hline 10 \end{array}$$

8.
$$\begin{array}{r} \square \\ -\ 15 \\ \hline 4 \end{array}$$

9.
$$\begin{array}{r} \square \\ -\ 15 \\ \hline 1 \end{array}$$

10.
$$\begin{array}{r} \square \\ -\ 15 \\ \hline 14 \end{array}$$

11.
$$\begin{array}{r} \square \\ -\ 15 \\ \hline 18 \end{array}$$

12.
$$\begin{array}{r} \square \\ -\ 15 \\ \hline 3 \end{array}$$

13.
$$\begin{array}{r} \square \\ -\ 15 \\ \hline 6 \end{array}$$

14.
$$\begin{array}{r} \square \\ -\ 15 \\ \hline 16 \end{array}$$

15.
$$\begin{array}{r} \square \\ -\ 15 \\ \hline 2 \end{array}$$

16.
$$\begin{array}{r} \square \\ -\ 15 \\ \hline 7 \end{array}$$

17.
$$\begin{array}{r} \square \\ -\ 15 \\ \hline 8 \end{array}$$

18.
$$\begin{array}{r} \square \\ -\ 15 \\ \hline 5 \end{array}$$

19.
$$\begin{array}{r} \square \\ -\ 15 \\ \hline 19 \end{array}$$

20.
$$\begin{array}{r} \square \\ -\ 15 \\ \hline 9 \end{array}$$

IF87115 *Timed Math Tests*

Subtraction Pretest

Name _____   Date _____

Time _____   Score _____

🕐 My time goal is _____ .

1. 31
   − 16

2. 34
   − 16

3. 16
   − 16

4. 29
   − 16

5. 17
   − 16

6. 20
   − 16

7. 33
   − 16

8. 18
   − 16

9. 25
   − 16

10. 21
    − 16

11. 23
    − 16

12. 26
    − 16

13. 30
    − 16

14. 22
    − 16

15. 27
    − 16

16. 32
    − 16

17. 19
    − 16

18. 28
    − 16

19. 35
    − 16

20. 24
    − 16

IF87115 *Timed Math Tests*

Subtraction/Addition Practice   −16B

Name _____   Date _____

Time _____   Score _____

My time goal is _____ .

1. 3
  $+ 16$

2. 17
  $- 16$

3. 25
  $- 16$

4. 14
  $+ 16$

5. 22
  $- 16$

6. 6
  $+ 16$

7. 20
  $- 16$

8. 7
  $+ 16$

9. 11
  $+ 16$

10. 21
  $- 16$

11. 18
  $- 16$

12. 11
  $+ 16$

13. 2
  $+ 16$

14. 19
  $- 16$

15. 12
  $+ 16$

16. 24
  $- 16$

17. 13
  $+ 16$

18. 23
  $- 16$

19. 4
  $+ 16$

20. 16
  $- 16$

IF87115 *Timed Math Tests*

Subtraction Challenge

Name _____   Date _____

Time _____   Score _____

⏰ My time goal is _____ .

1. □
    − 16
    ‾‾‾‾
    9

2. □
    − 16
    ‾‾‾‾
    19

3. □
    − 16
    ‾‾‾‾
    15

4. □
    − 16
    ‾‾‾‾
    8

5. □
    − 16
    ‾‾‾‾
    17

6. □
    − 16
    ‾‾‾‾
    2

7. □
    − 16
    ‾‾‾‾
    16

8. □
    − 16
    ‾‾‾‾
    6

9. □
    − 16
    ‾‾‾‾
    23

10. □
    − 16
    ‾‾‾‾
    18

11. □
    − 16
    ‾‾‾‾
    14

12. □
    − 16
    ‾‾‾‾
    21

13. □
    − 16
    ‾‾‾‾
    10

14. □
    − 16
    ‾‾‾‾
    4

15. □
    − 16
    ‾‾‾‾
    11

16. □
    − 16
    ‾‾‾‾
    7

17. □
    − 16
    ‾‾‾‾
    13

18. □
    − 16
    ‾‾‾‾
    20

19. □
    − 16
    ‾‾‾‾
    22

20. □
    − 16
    ‾‾‾‾
    12

IF87115 *Timed Math Tests*

Subtraction Pretest

Name _____   Date _____

Time _____   Score _____

🕐 My time goal is _____ .

1. 24 − 17	2. 19 − 17	3. 34 − 17	4. 26 − 17	5. 22 − 17
6. 30 − 17	7. 25 − 17	8. 29 − 17	9. 36 − 17	10. 23 − 17
11. 33 − 17	12. 31 − 17	13. 28 − 17	14. 17 − 17	15. 20 − 17
16. 35 − 17	17. 18 − 17	18. 27 − 17	19. 32 − 17	20. 21 − 17

114 IF87115 *Timed Math Tests*

Subtraction/Addition Practice

−17B

Name _____   Date _____

Time _____   Score _____

🕐 My time goal is _____ .

1.
$$8 + 17$$

2.
$$11 + 17$$

3.
$$18 - 17$$

4.
$$5 + 17$$

5.
$$20 - 17$$

6.
$$19 + 17$$

7.
$$21 - 17$$

8.
$$9 + 17$$

9.
$$17 - 17$$

10.
$$10 + 17$$

11.
$$28 - 17$$

12.
$$16 + 17$$

13.
$$33 - 17$$

14.
$$20 + 17$$

15.
$$14 + 17$$

16.
$$29 - 17$$

17.
$$24 - 17$$

18.
$$6 + 17$$

19.
$$13 + 17$$

20.
$$22 - 17$$

IF87115 *Timed Math Tests*

Subtraction Challenge

Name _____ Date _____

Time _____ Score _____

🕐 My time goal is _____ .

1.
$$\begin{array}{r} \square \\ -\ 17 \\ \hline 15 \end{array}$$

2.
$$\begin{array}{r} \square \\ -\ 17 \\ \hline 7 \end{array}$$

3.
$$\begin{array}{r} \square \\ -\ 17 \\ \hline 20 \end{array}$$

4.
$$\begin{array}{r} \square \\ -\ 17 \\ \hline 13 \end{array}$$

5.
$$\begin{array}{r} \square \\ -\ 17 \\ \hline 17 \end{array}$$

6.
$$\begin{array}{r} \square \\ -\ 17 \\ \hline 11 \end{array}$$

7.
$$\begin{array}{r} \square \\ -\ 17 \\ \hline 10 \end{array}$$

8.
$$\begin{array}{r} \square \\ -\ 17 \\ \hline 4 \end{array}$$

9.
$$\begin{array}{r} \square \\ -\ 17 \\ \hline 1 \end{array}$$

10.
$$\begin{array}{r} \square \\ -\ 17 \\ \hline 14 \end{array}$$

11.
$$\begin{array}{r} \square \\ -\ 17 \\ \hline 18 \end{array}$$

12.
$$\begin{array}{r} \square \\ -\ 17 \\ \hline 12 \end{array}$$

13.
$$\begin{array}{r} \square \\ -\ 17 \\ \hline 6 \end{array}$$

14.
$$\begin{array}{r} \square \\ -\ 17 \\ \hline 16 \end{array}$$

15.
$$\begin{array}{r} \square \\ -\ 17 \\ \hline 2 \end{array}$$

16.
$$\begin{array}{r} \square \\ -\ 17 \\ \hline 7 \end{array}$$

17.
$$\begin{array}{r} \square \\ -\ 17 \\ \hline 8 \end{array}$$

18.
$$\begin{array}{r} \square \\ -\ 17 \\ \hline 5 \end{array}$$

19.
$$\begin{array}{r} \square \\ -\ 17 \\ \hline 19 \end{array}$$

20.
$$\begin{array}{r} \square \\ -\ 17 \\ \hline 9 \end{array}$$

IF87115 *Timed Math Tests*

Subtraction Pretest

Name _____ Date _____

Time _____ Score _____

🕐 My time goal is _____ .

1. 34
  − 18

2. 27
  − 18

3. 21
  − 18

4. 29
  − 18

5. 35
  − 18

6. 20
  − 18

7. 24
  − 18

8. 38
  − 18

9. 23
  − 18

10. 25
   − 18

11. 32
   − 18

12. 37
   − 18

13. 28
   − 18

14. 22
   − 18

15. 26
   − 18

16. 30
   − 18

17. 36
   − 18

18. 19
   − 18

19. 33
   − 18

20. 31
   − 18

IF87115 *Timed Math Tests*

Subtraction/Addition Practice

−18B

Name _____ Date _____

Time _____ Score _____

🕐 My time goal is _____ .

1. $\begin{array}{r} 3 \\ +\ 18 \\ \hline \end{array}$	2. $\begin{array}{r} 37 \\ -\ 18 \\ \hline \end{array}$	3. $\begin{array}{r} 30 \\ -\ 18 \\ \hline \end{array}$	4. $\begin{array}{r} 14 \\ +\ 18 \\ \hline \end{array}$	5. $\begin{array}{r} 5 \\ +\ 18 \\ \hline \end{array}$
6. $\begin{array}{r} 23 \\ -\ 18 \\ \hline \end{array}$	7. $\begin{array}{r} 20 \\ +\ 18 \\ \hline \end{array}$	8. $\begin{array}{r} 25 \\ -\ 18 \\ \hline \end{array}$	9. $\begin{array}{r} 11 \\ +\ 18 \\ \hline \end{array}$	10. $\begin{array}{r} 21 \\ -\ 18 \\ \hline \end{array}$
11. $\begin{array}{r} 21 \\ +\ 18 \\ \hline \end{array}$	12. $\begin{array}{r} 22 \\ -\ 18 \\ \hline \end{array}$	13. $\begin{array}{r} 12 \\ +\ 18 \\ \hline \end{array}$	14. $\begin{array}{r} 19 \\ -\ 18 \\ \hline \end{array}$	15. $\begin{array}{r} 24 \\ -\ 18 \\ \hline \end{array}$
16. $\begin{array}{r} 32 \\ -\ 18 \\ \hline \end{array}$	17. $\begin{array}{r} 13 \\ +\ 18 \\ \hline \end{array}$	18. $\begin{array}{r} 26 \\ -\ 18 \\ \hline \end{array}$	19. $\begin{array}{r} 4 \\ +\ 18 \\ \hline \end{array}$	20. $\begin{array}{r} 30 \\ -\ 18 \\ \hline \end{array}$

IF87115 *Timed Math Tests*

Subtraction Challenge

Name _____   Date _____

Time _____   Score _____

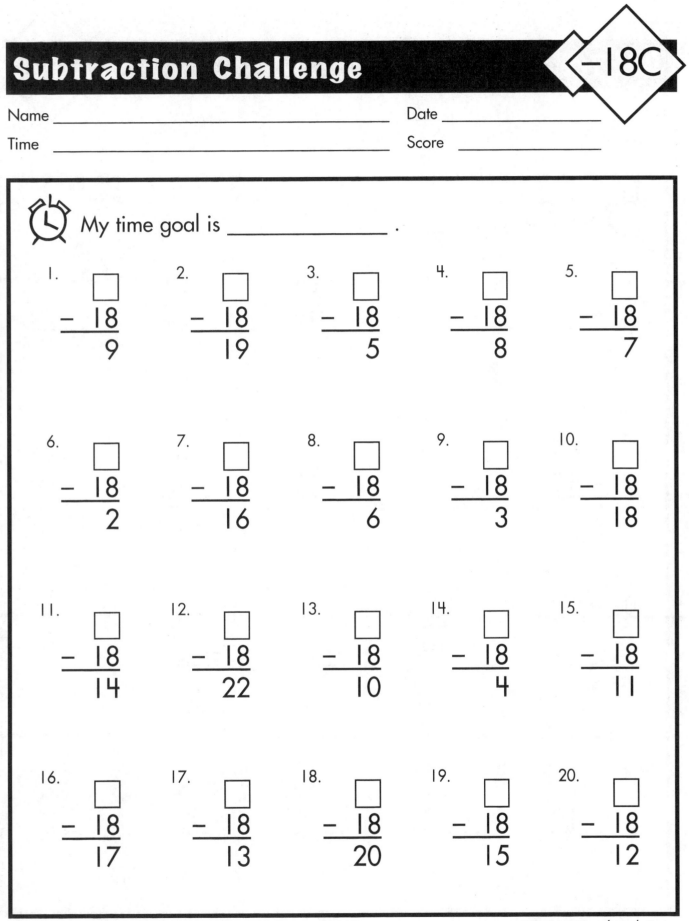

My time goal is _____ .

1.
☐
− 18
9

2.
☐
− 18
19

3.
☐
− 18
5

4.
☐
− 18
8

5.
☐
− 18
7

6.
☐
− 18
2

7.
☐
− 18
16

8.
☐
− 18
6

9.
☐
− 18
3

10.
☐
− 18
18

11.
☐
− 18
14

12.
☐
− 18
22

13.
☐
− 18
10

14.
☐
− 18
4

15.
☐
− 18
11

16.
☐
− 18
17

17.
☐
− 18
13

18.
☐
− 18
20

19.
☐
− 18
15

20.
☐
− 18
12

IF87115 *Timed Math Tests*

Subtraction Pretest

Name _____ Date _____

Time _____ Score _____

🕐 My time goal is _____ .

1. $\begin{array}{r} 28 \\ -\ 19 \\ \hline \end{array}$	2. $\begin{array}{r} 36 \\ -\ 19 \\ \hline \end{array}$	3. $\begin{array}{r} 31 \\ -\ 19 \\ \hline \end{array}$	4. $\begin{array}{r} 21 \\ -\ 19 \\ \hline \end{array}$	5. $\begin{array}{r} 26 \\ -\ 19 \\ \hline \end{array}$
6. $\begin{array}{r} 39 \\ -\ 19 \\ \hline \end{array}$	7. $\begin{array}{r} 34 \\ -\ 19 \\ \hline \end{array}$	8. $\begin{array}{r} 27 \\ -\ 19 \\ \hline \end{array}$	9. $\begin{array}{r} 38 \\ -\ 19 \\ \hline \end{array}$	10. $\begin{array}{r} 25 \\ -\ 19 \\ \hline \end{array}$
11. $\begin{array}{r} 32 \\ -\ 19 \\ \hline \end{array}$	12. $\begin{array}{r} 22 \\ -\ 19 \\ \hline \end{array}$	13. $\begin{array}{r} 29 \\ -\ 19 \\ \hline \end{array}$	14. $\begin{array}{r} 37 \\ -\ 19 \\ \hline \end{array}$	15. $\begin{array}{r} 20 \\ -\ 19 \\ \hline \end{array}$
16. $\begin{array}{r} 24 \\ -\ 19 \\ \hline \end{array}$	17. $\begin{array}{r} 33 \\ -\ 19 \\ \hline \end{array}$	18. $\begin{array}{r} 30 \\ -\ 19 \\ \hline \end{array}$	19. $\begin{array}{r} 35 \\ -\ 19 \\ \hline \end{array}$	20. $\begin{array}{r} 23 \\ -\ 19 \\ \hline \end{array}$

IF87115 *Timed Math Tests*

Subtraction/Addition Practice   −19B

Name _____   Date _____

Time _____   Score _____

My time goal is _____ .

1.
$$9$$
$$+ 19$$

2.
$$11$$
$$+ 19$$

3.
$$22$$
$$- 19$$

4.
$$20$$
$$- 19$$

5.
$$5$$
$$+ 19$$

6.
$$23$$
$$- 19$$

7.
$$15$$
$$+ 19$$

8.
$$26$$
$$- 19$$

9.
$$17$$
$$+ 19$$

10.
$$19$$
$$+ 19$$

11.
$$28$$
$$- 19$$

12.
$$16$$
$$+ 19$$

13.
$$25$$
$$- 19$$

14.
$$19$$
$$- 19$$

15.
$$4$$
$$+ 19$$

16.
$$24$$
$$- 19$$

17.
$$21$$
$$- 19$$

18.
$$6$$
$$+ 19$$

19.
$$30$$
$$- 19$$

20.
$$22$$
$$- 19$$

IF87115 *Timed Math Tests*

Subtraction Challenge

Name _____ Date _____

Time _____ Score _____

My time goal is _____ .

1.
$$\begin{array}{r} \square \\ -\ 19 \\ \hline 15 \end{array}$$

2.
$$\begin{array}{r} \square \\ -\ 19 \\ \hline 12 \end{array}$$

3.
$$\begin{array}{r} \square \\ -\ 19 \\ \hline 20 \end{array}$$

4.
$$\begin{array}{r} \square \\ -\ 19 \\ \hline 13 \end{array}$$

5.
$$\begin{array}{r} \square \\ -\ 19 \\ \hline 17 \end{array}$$

6.
$$\begin{array}{r} \square \\ -\ 19 \\ \hline 11 \end{array}$$

7.
$$\begin{array}{r} \square \\ -\ 19 \\ \hline 10 \end{array}$$

8.
$$\begin{array}{r} \square \\ -\ 19 \\ \hline 4 \end{array}$$

9.
$$\begin{array}{r} \square \\ -\ 19 \\ \hline 1 \end{array}$$

10.
$$\begin{array}{r} \square \\ -\ 19 \\ \hline 14 \end{array}$$

11.
$$\begin{array}{r} \square \\ -\ 19 \\ \hline 18 \end{array}$$

12.
$$\begin{array}{r} \square \\ -\ 19 \\ \hline 3 \end{array}$$

13.
$$\begin{array}{r} \square \\ -\ 19 \\ \hline 6 \end{array}$$

14.
$$\begin{array}{r} \square \\ -\ 19 \\ \hline 16 \end{array}$$

15.
$$\begin{array}{r} \square \\ -\ 19 \\ \hline 2 \end{array}$$

16.
$$\begin{array}{r} \square \\ -\ 19 \\ \hline 7 \end{array}$$

17.
$$\begin{array}{r} \square \\ -\ 19 \\ \hline 8 \end{array}$$

18.
$$\begin{array}{r} \square \\ -\ 19 \\ \hline 5 \end{array}$$

19.
$$\begin{array}{r} \square \\ -\ 19 \\ \hline 19 \end{array}$$

20.
$$\begin{array}{r} \square \\ -\ 19 \\ \hline 9 \end{array}$$

IF87115 *Timed Math Tests*

Subtraction/Addition Review

Name _____ Date _____

Time _____ Score _____

⏰ My time goal is _____ .

1. $\begin{array}{r}12\\+\ 4\\\hline\end{array}$	2. $\begin{array}{r}11\\+\ 5\\\hline\end{array}$	3. $\begin{array}{r}14\\-\ 4\\\hline\end{array}$	4. $\begin{array}{r}3\\-\ 2\\\hline\end{array}$	5. $\begin{array}{r}20\\+\ 4\\\hline\end{array}$
6. $\begin{array}{r}16\\-\ 2\\\hline\end{array}$	7. $\begin{array}{r}7\\+\ 4\\\hline\end{array}$	8. $\begin{array}{r}11\\-\ 2\\\hline\end{array}$	9. $\begin{array}{r}3\\+\ 5\\\hline\end{array}$	10. $\begin{array}{r}13\\+\ 3\\\hline\end{array}$
11. $\begin{array}{r}19\\-\ 6\\\hline\end{array}$	12. $\begin{array}{r}14\\+\ 4\\\hline\end{array}$	13. $\begin{array}{r}15\\-\ 5\\\hline\end{array}$	14. $\begin{array}{r}15\\-\ 4\\\hline\end{array}$	15. $\begin{array}{r}12\\+\ 5\\\hline\end{array}$
16. $\begin{array}{r}14\\+\ 2\\\hline\end{array}$	17. $\begin{array}{r}19\\-\ 3\\\hline\end{array}$	18. $\begin{array}{r}7\\+\ 6\\\hline\end{array}$	19. $\begin{array}{r}9\\+\ 3\\\hline\end{array}$	20. $\begin{array}{r}20\\+\ 5\\\hline\end{array}$

IF87115 *Timed Math Tests*

Subtraction/Addition Review

Name _____   Date _____

Time _____   Score _____

🕐 My time goal is _____ .

1.
$$18$$
$$+\ 7$$

2.
$$6$$
$$+\ 10$$

3.
$$14$$
$$-\ 11$$

4.
$$12$$
$$-\ 9$$

5.
$$11$$
$$-\ 8$$

6.
$$11$$
$$+\ 11$$

7.
$$20$$
$$-\ 10$$

8.
$$2$$
$$+\ 9$$

9.
$$18$$
$$-\ 11$$

10.
$$9$$
$$+\ 8$$

11.
$$6$$
$$+\ 7$$

12.
$$8$$
$$+\ 8$$

13.
$$12$$
$$-\ 8$$

14.
$$15$$
$$-\ 10$$

15.
$$11$$
$$-\ 9$$

16.
$$17$$
$$+\ 8$$

17.
$$19$$
$$-\ 8$$

18.
$$5$$
$$+\ 10$$

19.
$$7$$
$$+\ 7$$

20.
$$13$$
$$-\ 7$$

IF87115 *Timed Math Tests*

Subtraction/Addition Review

Name _____   Date _____

Time _____   Score _____

🕐 My time goal is _____ .

1.
$$\begin{array}{r} 19 \\ -\ 14 \\ \hline \end{array}$$

2.
$$\begin{array}{r} 19 \\ +\ 12 \\ \hline \end{array}$$

3.
$$\begin{array}{r} 24 \\ -\ 14 \\ \hline \end{array}$$

4.
$$\begin{array}{r} 15 \\ -\ 13 \\ \hline \end{array}$$

5.
$$\begin{array}{r} 19 \\ -\ 12 \\ \hline \end{array}$$

6.
$$\begin{array}{r} 8 \\ +\ 13 \\ \hline \end{array}$$

7.
$$\begin{array}{r} 18 \\ -\ 12 \\ \hline \end{array}$$

8.
$$\begin{array}{r} 14 \\ +\ 11 \\ \hline \end{array}$$

9.
$$\begin{array}{r} 15 \\ -\ 14 \\ \hline \end{array}$$

10.
$$\begin{array}{r} 20 \\ -\ 13 \\ \hline \end{array}$$

11.
$$\begin{array}{r} 12 \\ +\ 12 \\ \hline \end{array}$$

12.
$$\begin{array}{r} 15 \\ -\ 12 \\ \hline \end{array}$$

13.
$$\begin{array}{r} 14 \\ +\ 14 \\ \hline \end{array}$$

14.
$$\begin{array}{r} 12 \\ +\ 15 \\ \hline \end{array}$$

15.
$$\begin{array}{r} 17 \\ -\ 13 \\ \hline \end{array}$$

16.
$$\begin{array}{r} 19 \\ +\ 15 \\ \hline \end{array}$$

17.
$$\begin{array}{r} 17 \\ -\ 15 \\ \hline \end{array}$$

18.
$$\begin{array}{r} 16 \\ +\ 13 \\ \hline \end{array}$$

19.
$$\begin{array}{r} 14 \\ -\ 11 \\ \hline \end{array}$$

20.
$$\begin{array}{r} 6 \\ +\ 13 \\ \hline \end{array}$$

Subtraction/Addition Review

Name _____   Date _____

Time _____   Score _____

🕐 My time goal is _____ .

1. $\begin{array}{r} 19 \\ -\ 16 \\ \hline \end{array}$	2. $\begin{array}{r} 15 \\ +\ 17 \\ \hline \end{array}$	3. $\begin{array}{r} 18 \\ +\ 19 \\ \hline \end{array}$	4. $\begin{array}{r} 18 \\ -\ 16 \\ \hline \end{array}$	5. $\begin{array}{r} 19 \\ -\ 17 \\ \hline \end{array}$
6. $\begin{array}{r} 17 \\ -\ 17 \\ \hline \end{array}$	7. $\begin{array}{r} 8 \\ +\ 16 \\ \hline \end{array}$	8. $\begin{array}{r} 19 \\ +\ 19 \\ \hline \end{array}$	9. $\begin{array}{r} 13 \\ +\ 18 \\ \hline \end{array}$	10. $\begin{array}{r} 20 \\ -\ 17 \\ \hline \end{array}$
11. $\begin{array}{r} 9 \\ +\ 18 \\ \hline \end{array}$	12. $\begin{array}{r} 12 \\ +\ 18 \\ \hline \end{array}$	13. $\begin{array}{r} 4 \\ +\ 16 \\ \hline \end{array}$	14. $\begin{array}{r} 3 \\ +\ 20 \\ \hline \end{array}$	15. $\begin{array}{r} 20 \\ -\ 18 \\ \hline \end{array}$
16. $\begin{array}{r} 19 \\ -\ 19 \\ \hline \end{array}$	17. $\begin{array}{r} 8 \\ +\ 17 \\ \hline \end{array}$	18. $\begin{array}{r} 7 \\ +\ 19 \\ \hline \end{array}$	19. $\begin{array}{r} 16 \\ +\ 16 \\ \hline \end{array}$	20. $\begin{array}{r} 12 \\ +\ 16 \\ \hline \end{array}$

IF87115 *Timed Math Tests*

Answer Key

−2A
1, 5, 8, 2, 3,
16, 6, 18, 14, 0,
10, 4, 9, 7, 11,
17, 13, 10, 15, 12

−2B
21, 0, 8, 17, 6,
7, 9, 16, 7, 12,
18, 6, 9, 13, 15,
15, 18, 10, 16, 4

−2C
14, 17, 12, 15, 19,
13, 14, 12, 2, 6,
20, 8, 18, 5, 4,
9, 10, 7, 3, 11

−3A
12, 9, 3, 1, 6,
14, 0, 17, 11, 15,
2, 13, 4, 8, 5,
3, 7, 10, 16, 9

−3B
16, 0, 19, 10, 5,
17, 14, 9, 7, 22,
12, 14, 15, 16, 9,
7, 6, 10, 17, 2

−3C
12, 22, 8, 11, 10,
5, 19, 9, 6, 21,
17, 4, 13, 7, 14,
20, 16, 23, 18, 15

−4A
4, 15, 9, 6, 2,
7, 17, 3, 12, 1,
11, 18, 5, 13, 16,
10, 14, 7, 8, 19

−4B
12, 15, 14, 9, 16,
23, 4, 13, 13, 6,
14, 12, 9, 24, 8,
15, 10, 10, 17, 7

−4C
19, 16, 24, 17, 21,
15, 14, 8, 5, 18,
22, 7, 10, 20, 6,
11, 12, 9, 23, 13

−5A
10, 7, 1, 4, 12,
15, 9, 13, 0, 3,
11, 2, 6, 3, 1,
5, 8, 14, 7, 13

−5B
8, 12, 5, 19, 10,
8, 25, 2, 16, 3,
13, 6, 7, 24, 7,
10, 18, 15, 9, 11

−5C
13, 24, 10, 13, 12,
7, 21, 11, 8, 23,
19, 6, 15, 9, 16,
22, 18, 25, 20, 17

−6A
2, 13, 7, 4, 0,
5, 8, 1, 10, 3,
9, 6, 3, 11, 14,
8, 12, 5, 13, 4

−6B
18, 13, 7, 13, 26,
11, 24, 17, 25, 10,
4, 2, 8, 15, 12,
14, 5, 3, 14, 21

−6C
21, 18, 26, 19, 23,
17, 16, 10, 7, 20,
24, 9, 12, 22, 8,
13, 14, 11, 25, 15

−7A
8, 5, 9, 2, 10,
13, 7, 11, 8, 17,
16, 4, 1, 15, 3,
6, 12, 5, 11, 14

−7B
10, 10, 3, 21, 2,
13, 27, 14, 18, 14,
11, 4, 9, 12, 5,
8, 20, 16, 11, 23

−7C
16, 26, 22, 15, 24,
9, 23, 13, 30, 25,
21, 28, 17, 11, 18,
14, 20, 27, 29, 19

−8A
17, 11, 5, 2, 14,
3, 16, 18, 8, 15,
7, 4, 1, 9, 12,
6, 10, 3, 11, 13

−8B
16, 19, 10, 13, 12,
27, 13, 17, 9, 2,
10, 8, 5, 28, 22,
11, 6, 14, 21, 3

−8C
23, 20, 28, 21, 25,
19, 18, 12, 9, 22,
26, 11, 14, 24, 10,
15, 16, 13, 27, 17

−9A
6, 3, 12, 0, 8,
11, 5, 9, 14, 16,
7, 15, 2, 13, 17,
1, 4, 10, 3, 9

−9B
12, 8, 1, 23, 14,
4, 29, 8, 20, 12,
9, 2, 21, 10, 3,
6, 22, 5, 13, 7

−9C
18, 28, 14, 17, 16,
11, 25, 15, 12, 27,
23, 10, 19, 13, 20,
26, 22, 29, 24, 21

−10A
5, 2, 16, 8, 14,
11, 7, 13, 10, 4,
3, 6, 17, 1, 18,
15, 0, 3, 9, 12

−10B
9, 13, 6, 23, 4,
7, 28, 10, 14, 29,
5, 21, 8, 11, 16,
20, 31, 17, 2, 13

−10C
19, 29, 15, 18, 17,
12, 26, 16, 12, 28,
24, 11, 20, 14, 21,
27, 23, 30, 25, 22

−11A
17, 8, 2, 10, 15,
0, 3, 16, 5, 14,
4, 11, 18, 6, 9,
13, 7, 19, 1, 12

−11B
19, 22, 7, 9, 16,
12, 29, 15, 6, 8,
7, 5, 2, 30, 15,
13, 3, 17, 24, 10

−11C
26, 23, 31, 24, 28,
22, 21, 15, 12, 25,
29, 14, 17, 27, 13,
18, 19, 16, 30, 20

−12A
3, 0, 4, 17, 5,
8, 2, 6, 13, 9,
11, 14, 18, 10, 15,
1, 7, 16, 6, 12

−12B
15, 5, 13, 26, 10,
18, 8, 19, 23, 9,
6, 23, 14, 7, 24,
3, 25, 11, 16, 4

−12C
21, 31, 27, 20, 29,
14, 28, 18, 35, 30,
26, 33, 22, 16, 23,
19, 25, 32, 34, 24

−13A
11, 6, 0, 13, 9,
17, 12, 16, 3, 10,
2, 18, 15, 4, 7,
1, 5, 14, 19, 8

−13B
21, 24, 5, 18, 7,
32, 8, 22, 4, 23,
15, 3, 20, 33, 27,
16, 11, 19, 26, 9

IF87115 *Timed Math Tests*

Answer Key

-13C
28, 25, 33, 26, 30,
24, 23, 17, 14, 27,
31, 16, 19, 29, 15,
20, 21, 18, 32, 22

-14A
1, 13, 7, 15, 3,
6, 0, 4, 9, 11,
18, 10, 14, 8, 12,
16, 4, 5, 2, 17

-14B
17, 3, 6, 28, 19,
9, 34, 3, 25, 7,
4, 8, 26, 5, 10,
1, 27, 12, 18, 16

-14C
23, 33, 19, 22, 21,
16, 30, 20, 17, 32,
28, 15, 24, 18, 25,
31, 27, 34, 29, 26

-15A
13, 4, 16, 6, 11,
3, 19, 12, 1, 10,
0, 7, 14, 2, 5,
9, 18, 15, 20, 8

-15B
23, 26, 3, 5, 20,
8, 0, 11, 2, 4,
13, 1, 10, 4, 19,
9, 6, 21, 28, 7

-15C
30, 27, 35, 28, 32,
26, 25, 19, 16, 29,
33, 18, 21, 31, 17,
22, 23, 20, 34, 24

-16A
15, 18, 0, 13, 1,
4, 17, 2, 9, 5,
7, 10, 14, 6, 11,
16, 3, 12, 19, 8

-16B
19, 1, 9, 30, 6,
22, 4, 23, 27, 5,
2, 27, 18, 3, 28,
8, 29, 7, 20, 0

-16C
25, 35, 31, 24, 33,
18, 32, 22, 39, 34,
30, 37, 26, 20, 27,
23, 29, 36, 38, 28

-17A
7, 2, 17, 9, 5,
13, 8, 12, 19, 6,
16, 14, 11, 0, 3,
18, 1, 10, 15, 4

-17B
25, 28, 1, 22, 3,
36, 4, 26, 0, 27,
11, 33, 16, 37, 31,
12, 7, 23, 30, 5

-17C
32, 24, 37, 30, 34,
28, 27, 21, 18, 31,
35, 29, 23, 33, 19,
24, 25, 22, 36, 26

-18A
16, 9, 3, 11, 17,
2, 6, 20, 5, 7,
14, 19, 10, 4, 8,
12, 18, 1, 15, 13

-18B
21, 19, 12, 32, 23,
5, 38, 7, 29, 3,
39, 4, 30, 1, 6,
14, 31, 8, 22, 12

-18C
27, 37, 23, 26, 25,
20, 34, 24, 21, 36,
32, 40, 28, 22, 29,
35, 31, 38, 33, 30

-19A
9, 17, 12, 2, 7,
20, 15, 8 19, 6,
13, 3, 10, 18, 1,
5, 14, 11, 16, 4

-19B
28, 30, 3, 1, 24,
4, 34, 7, 36, 38,
9, 35, 6, 0, 23,
5, 2, 25, 11, 3

-19C
34, 31, 39, 32, 36,
30, 29, 23, 20, 33,
37, 22, 25, 35, 21,
26, 27, 24, 38, 28

Review A
16, 16, 10, 1, 24,
14, 11, 9, 8, 16,
13, 18, 10, 11, 17,
16, 16, 13, 12, 25

Review B
25, 16, 3, 3, 3,
22, 10, 11, 7, 17,
13, 16, 4, 5, 2,
25, 11, 15, 14, 6

Review C
5, 31, 10, 2, 7,
21, 6, 25, 1, 7,
24, 3, 28, 27, 4,
34, 2, 29, 3, 19

Review D
3, 32, 37, 2, 2,
0, 24, 38, 31, 3,
27, 30, 20, 23, 2,
0, 25, 26, 32, 28

IF87115 *Timed Math Tests*